EFFECTIVE TERM PAPERS AND REPORTS

COLES EDITORIAL BOARD

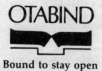

Bound to stay open

Publisher's Note

Otabind (Ota-bind). This book has been bound using the patented Otabind process. You can open this book at any page, gently run your finger down the spine, and the pages will lie flat.

ABOUT COLES NOTES

COLES NOTES have been an indispensible aid to students on five continents since 1948.

COLES NOTES are available for a wide range of individual literary works. Clear, concise explanations and insights are provided along with interesting interpretations and evaluations.

Proper use of COLES NOTES will allow the student to pay greater attention to lectures and spend less time taking notes. This will result in a broader understanding of the work being studied and will free the student for increased participation in discussions.

COLES NOTES are an invaluable aid for review and exam preparation as well as an invitation to explore different interpretive paths.

COLES NOTES are written by experts in their fields. It should be noted that any literary judgement expressed herein is just that — the judgement of one school of thought. Interpretations that diverge from, or totally disagree with any criticism may be equally valid.

COLES NOTES are designed to supplement the text and are not intended as a substitute for reading the text itself. Use of the NOTES will serve not only to clarify the work being studied, but should enhance the reader's enjoyment of the topic.

ISBN 0-7740-3429-7

© COPYRIGHT 1996 AND PUBLISHED BY
COLES PUBLISHING COMPANY
TORONTO—CANADA
PRINTED IN CANADA

Manufactured by Webcom Limited
Cover finish: Webcom's Exclusive **Duracoat**

CONTENTS

ABOUT THE AUTHOR

Lynda Hungerford
has taught composition and literature
since 1966
with a two-year break in between
to complete her own dissertation on the Middle English lyric.
She is now teaching at Illinois State University.
In addition to her academic career,
she has served as a consultant
to the authors' agency, Porter, Gould & Dierks,
in manuscript evaluation, for over five years.
She and her husband, also an academic, have two small boys.

ONE — RESEARCH AND WRITING

Introduction

Some people undertake an ambitious research project with unmixed enthusiasm. Experience has taught them that they have the knowledge of libraries and bibliographies, the intellectual strength, and the writing ability to see a project through to a happy end. Others undertake such a project with unmixed dread; they don't like doing library research, and they either do not like to write or feel they cannot do so well. The first fortunate group have no need for a guide, and it is hoped that the second will not put themselves in a position which requires one. Most, however, begin such projects hoping that once finished, they will be pleased with their work, but knowing that there will be false starts and frustrations. They may even fear their enthusiasm will so wane that they may end with a half-hearted effort or even quit. This guide is intended to help them reduce false starts and frustrations and to provide knowledge of research and writing techniques needed to produce a report which represents their best work.

A research project for an advanced course or degree needs to satisfy someone other than the writer himself. It must meet the standards of an instructor or director. Although such standards may include an idiosyncrasy or two, there are many common standards by which reports are evaluated. First, the report should present complete and valid data. Second, it should bear evidence of the writer's having weighed and measured the work of others on the subject. Third, its arguments and interpretations should be at least tenable and at best demonstrably valid. Finally, the report should have a strong informing principle, that is, a principle of organization provided by the author.

This guide can provide some direct help in meeting these standards. First, you will acquire and verify much if not all of your data in the library, and the guide describes what kind of data you might find in what kind of library and the easiest way of getting it. Some of the arguments and interpretations you present will be your own, some will be those of other scholars, and the guide can help you find the work of other scholars and show you the ways you can legitimately use their work. On the other hand, your evaluation of the work of others and the construction of arguments and interpretations of your own depend on your understanding of the discipline within which your project falls. Thus, if your project involves evaluating a social scientist's argument based on a statistical survey, you will need a knowledge of the valid use of surveys and statistics, knowledge beyond the scope of this guide. After all, research projects are routinely assigned to give the student a chance to show how he can apply the principles he has learned to an independent project. Many of those principles are specific to the subject and thus are not to be found in a general guide to research.

As for the organizing principle, the guide discusses some of the ways authors arrive at one for their work, but that principle must come from the writer, that is, from the powers of your mind and imagination. Those powers will have been heightened by what you have learned about the discipline and what you have discovered in your research, but in the end they are your own.

So far, however, we have talked only about the substance of the report. The form remains. While a discussion can leave the form and substance tidily separate, such an abstraction is misleading. Bad writing is confusing and unconvincing. Since the reader has only the written report, he cannot be expected to discriminate between an argument which is bad because it is poorly thought out and one which is merely sloppily presented. Indeed, the two often go together. An argument is likely to be badly written because it has been poorly thought out, and a poorly thought out argument is bound to appear so in writing. A few scholars have distinctive styles which actually add to their work, but for the apprentice in research writing, the best prose style is probably a self-effacing style, which instead of drawing attention to itself presents arguments in a clear, convincing way, and this guide describes the processes of revision which create such a style. Adding the characteristics of an especially incisive mind or quick wit is beyond our scope.

Prose style is not the only element of form in a research report. Documentation, that is, the use of footnotes and bibliographic information to support assertions and arguments, is a second element. The reader expects to know at a glance where he must go to check the accuracy of a fact or of an opinion attributed to another scholar. The reader can know this only if he and the author share an understanding of what goes into a footnote and where. So the guide includes information about the standard forms of footnoting and presenting bibliographic information in the text and bibliography.

The form given in this guide for the arrangement of information in the footnote and bibliography is the fullest form in use today and the one that has the widest acceptance, for it is used throughout the humanities. Mastering this form will put the student in sufficient command of the details of bibliography that he will easily adapt to any of the several forms used in the social and natural sciences. He will know, for example, what constitutes a full author entry, what to do with a corporate author, and the difference between a new edition and a reprint. Such knowledge makes the superficial rearrangement of the information a minor problem. Thus, once the student knows how to determine the correct date of publication, it is a simple matter for him to put it after the place of publication or the name of the publisher, according to the demands of his particular field.

We cannot and will not try to provide a formula by which someone can effortlessly or thoughtlessly produce a good report. There is no such formula. Neither good research nor good writing comes easily, and a report of any sort is almost certainly doomed if the writer is unwilling to devote sufficient time and energy to the project. But the addition of know-how to diligence does save time, energy, and frustration. For example, if you make a complete bibliography card the first time, you will not find yourself frustrated by having to go back to the library to verify a page number or an edition number only to discover that the book is out on loan or lost. The techniques presented here will not guarantee that you will not find your best lead in a totally unexpected place, that you will not suffer a sudden attack of writer's block, or that your typist's toddler won't cast your footnotes into the fireplace. We hope that the techniques will, however, divert you from paths that lead inevitably to frustration.

Some kinds of frustration can be avoided, but not all, simply because writing is more than a stimulus response pattern, and, therefore, writing a research report is creative. Two people following the same approach will not always perceive the same facts, and having found the facts they will not interpret them the same way. Looking at a field of daffodils does not elicit a poem from all of us, and "I Wandered Lonely as A Cloud" is a unique poetic response to a field of daffodils. Likewise, assuming legend trustworthy, many observed apples falling before Newton described gravity. Although logic as well as the standards of an academic discipline prescribe limits for a research report, within those limits the mind is free to discover, or to fail to discover, patterns and relationships.

The techniques of research given here are designed to suggest routines to minimize the thought given to the uncreative aspects of research. None of us can afford the time it takes to track down the quotation we forgot to document in our notes. Such a task can take several days of unproductive time going over books and articles already surveyed. Mental notes are easily forgotten, and making a point of remembering something rather than writing it down invites confusion and frantic re-researching. Most of us have time for only one round of research. Thus, by establishing a routine in which we always document a note in the same unambiguous way, we leave ourselves free to devote most of our conscious thinking to the interesting problems encountered in our reading. Tedium cannot be eliminated, but it can be reduced. Intellectual creativity, on the other hand, cannot be forced, but it can be encouraged.

WHAT MUST BE DONE

The assumption that the research paper involves creativity will not alter dramatically the four steps usually prescribed for research reports: (1) choice of a subject, (2) research, reading, and note-taking, (3) writing, and (4) revising. But here the steps are given with the warning that the four activities do not go on in pristine isolation, but are, instead, intimately related. Often your research will show good and sound reason for altering an early conception of your topic. Often too the act of writing will reveal a gap in the research which must be filled by more research and reading. Finally, ideas exist only as they are expressed, and in a written work that means they exist in the language in which they are stated. Thus, you define the limits of your topic even as you revise the final draft.

The interrelationship of the four steps of research can be seen in a hypothetical example. A student choosing a subject might decide that he wanted to study the Middle English lyric. After reading several anthologies of Middle English lyrics, he might decide to limit his reading to the religious lyric and after reading many such lyrics and perhaps several books about them, he might then conclude that the penitential lyric of the fourteenth century provided a subject with manageable boundaries, with possibilities for original analysis, and for which he had access to the relevant library resources. He could feel confident that he had a sound topic, but the confidence would be possible only because he had done some of his reading and bibliographical work.

Our hypothetical researcher had to avoid two dangers in selecting a topic: (1) selecting a topic so broad that he exhausted his research time before he mastered it, and (2) limiting himself early in his work to a topic on which he would exhaust his time trying to ferret out non-existent material. By far the greater of the two dangers is postponing narrowing the topic. At the doctoral level, a prospectus, or description of proposed research, usually must be approved before a student's topic is accepted. Even at this advanced level, and even with graduate instructors in general agreement that the prospectus is closer to a hunting license than a description of exactly what prize will be brought home, the most common reason for rejecting a prospectus is that the topic is too broad. One can stake out an acre or so in hopes of finding gold; one cannot stake out the whole of California. Sooner or later the prospector has to give up his airborne scanning of the landscape and begin to dig. He may not find gold when he does dig, but he most certainly won't find it from the airplane. Fortunately for the researcher, a rigorous examination of some aspect of his subject is much more likely to yield new insights than mining the average rock is likely to yield gold. The principle is the same for any research project, whether or not the researcher must have his topic formally approved or not; the sooner he narrows the topic, the less time he spends on peripheral reading and research.

The ideal subject is narrow enough to be examined completely within the scope of your time and ambition. You will also have to appraise realistically the resources of the libraries available to you, for to put together a short report of twenty-five pages or so you will need two or three books basic to your subject and some additional material — chapters from other books, articles in periodicals, or the results of original field work and experiments. Research does not, of course, end with this material; it begins with it. The basic core will probably contain bibliographical material that you will want to follow out, and when discrepancies show up, you will need to consult other works to resolve them. In addition you will have to search bibliographies in the library to discover less obvious sources that might directly bear on your topic. But without the basic core of four or five sources at hand you have no beginning.

As you narrow your topic and read your basic books and articles, you develop your bibliography and take notes. To develop the bibliography you record, either by listing or on separate cards, references, books and articles which you will want to examine in the course of your research. Typically, notes contain the factual information, interpretations, and arguments which you will examine in the report, and they can be taken in a variety of ways. Some people prefer larger note cards with one note to a card. Some people prefer notebooks, or large sheets of paper. Note cards are flexible because they can be shuffled and rearranged easily. But notes in notebooks are easier to carry and harder to lose than separate cards. Also, a notebook sheet allows for a more complex or extensive note, though for the inexperienced or undisciplined researcher, that can, as we shall see later, be a temptation to postpone the intellectual work that should go into note-taking. The sooner you establish a routine for yourself in regard to how you take notes, the more distractions you will eliminate from your work.

When you have taken notes on a significant portion of your research you can and should begin writing, even though the research writer is sometimes advised to complete his note—taking before writing. That is a fine idea if you are secure in your ability to pace yourself and have done your research so thoroughly that discrepancies in fact or gaps in argument do not appear when you begin to write. For many people, however, writing is an internal dialogue which reveals the exact subject and the arguments related to it. In addition, experience is needed to gage accurately the number of words needed to express an idea or couch an argument. The sentence that you thought would easily expand to fill several pages, sits before you still a sentence, an important one, but a sentence nevertheless. The point that you thought might take a paragraph to develop may take several pages of expansion and development to be clear. Most important, the ideas that are foggily in the back of your mind for inclusion may, when you get down to expressing them clearly, not look nearly as interesting to you, or they may need more rigorous examination and working out before they can be included. The sooner you express your ideas on paper the sooner you can examine and evaluate them. So, if it is possible to work up the research on separate aspect of your subject, do so. Then you can begin writing on one aspect while you pursue the research on another.

When your research is complete and you have followed out all the pertinent leads on your subject, then you will want to finish a preliminary draft as soon as possible. If you have written a few sections or done other forms of preliminary writing while you were doing your research, this task will seem less formidable. It will be easier too, if in writing the subsections you have developed something of a routine for writing. For your first draft you may have prepared an outline in advance or you may simply have jotted down the subtopics of your subject and the order in which you plan to treat them. Ready and easy guides to writing usually prescribe outlines, but the more creatively you are working with organizing your material the less likely you are to produce a tidy outline, since the organizing principles have to be clearly in mind to make the outline. Moreover, struggling with the outline may just be a way of postponing writing. Revising and refining an outline is not a substitute for beginning to write.

Once you begin your first draft, press through to the end. You can afford to be sloppy with grammar and diction. You can afford even to leave blanks when you can't think of any word that would do or when you discover you don't know an important date or name. Once you have begun the first draft, the highest priority is to finish it, and you can afford to be sloppy because when you finish the first draft you begin to revise.

Rewriting is absolutely essential, and it is the step that inexperienced writers and harried students are most likely to try to eliminate or to scrimp on. Good, responsible writers just don't let first drafts go unrevised into the world. The revising of a research paper involves weighing the arguments anew, examining the order of presentation of subtopics and ideas to see if some other arrangement would be more effective, verifying names, dates, quotations and facts, and, finally, seeing that the words into which all is put are the clearest and most direct possible,

All of these steps take time. Surely everyone knows that he is supposed to budget his time. For research and writing most of us need to budget liberally. One graduate instructor has commented, "The secret vice of every graduate student is optimism." At the time he was examining the projected dates of completion of dissertations. That the vice prevails far beyond the final stages of graduate work is attested to by the innumerable papers sloppily finished in the early morning hours of the due date. To have to begin writing when you know you have not gotten to some relevant sources is debilitating. How can you confidently pursue your argument when you know you have examined only some of the evidence? Failure to rewrite will simply muddle your work and may result in your best ideas going unrecognized and unrewarded. To avoid such traps, realistically assume that every phase of your work will take longer than you expect and plan accordingly.

There are, then, four steps in the research project: choosing the subject, research and note-taking, writing, and revising. The first two steps will bring you to the library, and the kind of library you have available will help to determine the procedures you follow in your research.

LIBRARIES

The large research library of a major university attempts to buy every scholarly book by a reputable publisher and to acquire all scholarly journals. Your problem in such a library is to find in a mass of two to ten million books those few that are relevant to your particular topic.

A special library is one that is devoted to one or several particular fields. The John Crerar Library now at Illinois Institute of Technology has over a million volumes on scientific and technical subjects. Thus, although it has fewer volumes than the more academically oriented libraries of Northwestern University and the University of Chicago, it might well have more thorough coverage of some technical subjects, such as architecture. A special library may have specific limitations. The library of the American Medical Association, for example, tries to maintain complete world coverage of journals in clinical medicine, but it has not retained most journals before 1962; hence its collection would be most useful for recent material. Another example is the Huntington Library and Art Gallery, which is devoted to rare books and modern English and American first editions. Special libraries often have reference sections which are broader in scope than their general collection of books and periodicals, and which can be used for verification of facts outside the field of special interest and, perhaps, for bibliographic purposes.

In addition, some libraries maintain special collections. For example, Northwestern University maintains a separate, large collection of materials relating to African history, literature, and linguistics. The Directory of Special Libraries and Information Centers, edited by Anthony T. Kruzas (Detroit: Gale, 1968) has an index in which you may be able to locate a special library or special collection covering your subject. In the directory, for example, you could learn that the Illinois State Historical Library in Springfield is one of several libraries with a special collection devoted to Mormon history.

If you are lucky enough to know the author or title of a good general book on your subject, you are almost certain to find it in the stacks of a major research library or a special library in your field, and you can begin your reading and bibliographic search with that book. If your topic is narrow enough and if the subject catalog of the library is detailed enough, you may be able to find two or three relevant books through the subject catalog, and those books can provide your beginning leads. However, if your topic is at all general, you will soon discover that the library has an unmanageable number of books on the subject, and you will need to begin work in the reference room.

An undergraduate college library may be a carefully selected collection of the hundred thousand or so books deemed most useful for the research projects of undergraduates. Such libraries usually belong to major universities which also have graduate research libraries or to a very select few of the best and oldest undergraduate colleges. In such a library you can proceed as in a university research library with the additional advantage that you are unlikely to be overwhelmed by the sheer volume of material. Unfortunately most undergraduate colleges have libraries which, like Topsy, just grew. Hence their collections are likely to be lopsided and patchy. The number and kind of books in a particular field may well be determined by the interests of particular faculty members. Moreover, a thousand of its 33,000 volumes may have been donated by the local minister in 1929 and reflect his passionate interest in marble effigies or African ceremonial masks. In such a library you are probably best off beginning your research in the reference room, especially if the solid general book you had hoped to find in the library is not there.

Public libraries, with rare exceptions like the New York Public Library, are not intended to serve in-depth research. If you must work in an ordinary public library, you will be more limited than in an even modest college library, and you will have to expect to depend on interlibrary loan and other tedious procedures. Even the reference collection is likely to be disappointing. Before accepting such limitations, at least explore the possibility of using a nearby college or university library.

THE REFERENCE ROOM

The reference collection of any library is used for several purposes. You can find direction there to the general works you need to read before narrowing your subject and to the best basic works in your field. When your subject is further defined you can return to the reference room for a thorough bibliographic search for relevant materials, and, in the case of a dissertation, to guarantee that your project has not been done, or not been done adequately, before. The reference room also provides specific facts and information you need for your project, for example the date when the rosary took its present form, the population of London after the great fire, or the source of a literary quotation or allusion.

A number of guides to reference books are available, some of them in inexpensive paperbacks. Constance Winchell's *Guide to Reference Books,* 8th ed. (Chicago: American Library Association, 1967) with its three supplements compiled by Eugene P. Sheehy (1968, 1970, 1972) is an extensive guide to reference material published before 1970 and should be available in any library. Winchell's *Guide* is organized by subject and then by class of reference work (bibliography, guide, handbook, etc.), and it includes descriptive comments from a few sentences to several paragraphs in length. For example, of Richard D. Altick and Andrew Wright's *Selective Bibliography for the Study of English and American Literature,* 2nd ed. (New York: Macmillan,

1963) she says, "A highly selective guide to research materials; classified arrangement with author, title, and subject index."

In addition to directing students to bibliographical material and handbooks, reference guides such as Winchell, Frances Neel Cheney's *Fundamental Reference Sources* (Chicago: American Library Association, 1971) or Mona McCormick's *The New York Times Guide to Reference Materials* (New York: Popular Library, 1971) can direct you to the most appropriate encyclopedias, almanacs, statistical abstracts, or dictionaries for verifying or discovering specific facts. When, in your search for a particular fact, your ingenuity combined with the information in such guides fails, the reference librarian may be able to help you find the right source.

THE GROWTH OF A BIBLIOGRAPHY

At the beginning of a project you want quick direction to the best basic books. Such books can be found directly in Winchell, or in the guides and handbooks to various subjects that she cites, such as Frederick Bateson's *A Guide to English Literature,* 2nd ed. (Chicago: Aldine, 1967), or a history of the subject, such as *The Oxford History of South Africa,* edited by Monica Hunter Wilson and Leonard Thompson, 2 vols. (New York: Oxford University Press, 1969-71). If the broader subject is limited to a particular individual, a biography or biographical dictionary might provide leads to basic material. Occasionally encyclopedias can be used for preliminary research, but it should be remembered that encyclopedias have distinct limitations and are not entitled to awed respect. Articles for encyclopedias are necessarily finished long before the encyclopedia is published, so that the information is not usually current even with the date of publication. Moreover, the articles are brief and seldom prepared with the care that goes into a book or journal article which will prominently display the author's name. Sometimes, too, encyclopedia articles are left unrevised or are only partially revised for new editions.

You go to a guide or handbook, a history of your subject, or an annotated bibliography to find the titles of the best books and articles related to the aspect which interests you. You go to such guides rather than to a comprehensive bibliography in your field so that you will learn early in your research the books and articles which are judged by scholars in the field to be significant and accurate. The fear of reading a masterly work on the subject because it might leave you with nothing to say or prejudice your judgments should pale into insignificance beside the possibility of being seduced into a dead-end investigation by the meanderings of an ill-informed writer or crank.

In addition to providing references to what becomes the basis of the research, the guide, history, or handbook may provide additional leads to useful books and articles. These references, of course, will be noted down as they are found on bibliography cards. A bibliography card is usually a three by five inch card containing the information needed to find the book and all of the information needed for a bibliographic entry in the final paper.

A complete card for a book might look like this:

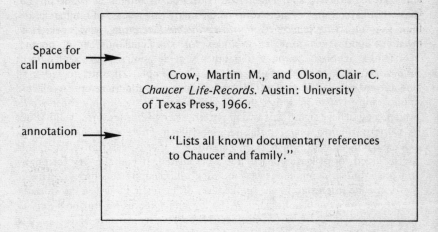

Space for
call number

Crow, Martin M., and Olson, Clair C.
Chaucer Life-Records. Austin: University
of Texas Press, 1966.

annotation

"Lists all known documentary references
to Chaucer and family."

Of course you may choose any size card or slip of paper you like, but you must be consistent about how you arrange information on the card so that you can automatically retrieve it. If you are inconsistent, you may find yourself wondering if Henry Regnery is the editor or publisher. An omission on the bibliography card will usually entail an extra trip to the library to recover the missing information. It may seem like a short cut to note merely the author and title for a book, but if the book must be ordered from a bookseller or requested on interlibrary loan, complete bibliographical information is essential. If all the information you need is not given in your source, leave ample room to add it in the appropriate place on the card. The blank spaces will remind you to write down the information when you do find it, and preparing your bibliography will be easier if all the cards follow the same pattern. A list on a sheet of paper is less convenient than a pack of individual cards because the entries on the list cannot be reorganized and references cannot be easily discarded.

Once the subject of the report has been narrowed down sufficiently, you are ready to do a thorough bibliographical search to find references to all the material which bears on your subject, or at least to as much of it as you can cover before the project is due. In the case of a doctoral dissertation the search must ensure that you are not duplicating the work of another scholar. Indeed, any researcher wants to find the place where he can begin to build on the firm work of others and thus, in his more or less ambitious way, expand the frontiers of knowledge.

To expand and supplement the collection of references found in your basic books you may explore some of the many other kinds of bibliographies. For example, *The Readers' Guide to Periodical Literature* (New York: H.W. Wilson, 1900—date) provides an index for a selected number of popular manazines. Scholarly journals sometimes provide annual indexes of current books and articles in the field. *PMLA*, for example, attempts to index all the current scholarly work on all modern languages and literature. A selected bibliography is one in which the compilers have included only those works which they believe significant and important. "English Literature, 1660-1800: A Current Bibliography," published annually in *Philological Quarterly*, is a selected bibliography which is also annotated; that is, descriptive comments are included for at least some of the works listed. If you are very fortunate, you may find a comprehensive annotated bibliography covering your topic. For someone interested in the application of linguistic theory to the study of literature, for example, Richard W. Bailey and Dolores M. Burton's *English Stylistics: A Bibliography* (Cambridge: Massachusetts Institute of Technology Press, 1968) provides such a tool.

It is a rare research project, indeed, for which a search of just one or two bibliographies will guarantee thorough coverage. A good handbook or guide should help you assemble a list of sources of bibliographical information in your field. To make sure that you are getting the coverage you need, check for each bibliography you use the material surveyed for the bibliography and the cutoff dates for inclusion. For example, some bibliographies include dissertations and some do not. The *PMLA* bibliography looks deceptively comprehensive, but before 1956 it is limited to works by American scholars, so that the earlier bibliographies must be supplemented by other bibliographies which cover work by non-American scholars.

Rather than consult annual bibliographies of current publications over a long period of years, try to find a bibliography which covers a long period of time in your field, such as the Bailey and Burton bibliography of style. As a general rule, it is wise to begin with the bibliography that is most closely confined to your subject and, if possible, to begin with an annotated bibliography. Thus, for a project on Wordsworth, a student who consulted either Winchell or Bateson's *Guide to English Literature* would learn of Elton F. Henley and David Stom's *Wordsworthian Criticism, 1945-1964: An Annotated Bibliography*, rev. ed. (New York: New York Public Library, 1965). It is obviously preferable to consult this single 107-page volume than to plod through twenty to thirty-two separate annual bibliographies of English literature. Of course Henley and Stom would have to be supplemented to cover the period after 1964. This could be done through "The Romantic Movement: A Selective and Critical Bibliography" published annually in *English Language Notes*, 1964-date, or in the *PMLA* bibliography.

There is no point in searching for bibliographical references you will not have time to read or even acquire. For most researchers this means that a standard selected annotated bibliography is more useful than culling many comprehensive bibliographies which include material that is of doubtful value and available only in the largest libraries. It takes at least four to six weeks, for example, to acquire a dissertation on microfilm or in photocopy form, and the time for interlibrary loan can be even longer. Even the dissertation author who must prove that his work is original is better off using a limited bibliography, doing his preliminary reading, and narrowing his subject as much as possible before doing the comprehensive search. To copy down all of the bibliographical entries pertinent to Wordsworth is a futile exercise of the worst sort. There is no way you can read everything before the seminar paper is due, the dissertation deadline has passed and left you in permanent academic peonage, or your publisher has found someone else to do the book.

Your goal should be to have a small, carefully selected pack of bibliography cards all of which are pertinent to your narrow, defined subject. This scant, unpretentious list of books will grow as you pursue your work and ask questions of your own that entail going to sources not previously applied to your subject; the answers to those questions may well be the heart of your paper. Keep in mind that the research paper is not an exercise in making a long bibliographical list, nor is it designed to show that you have read a lot of books. At whatever level you are working, the goal is to assemble and present true, verifiable information in a way in which it has not been assembled and presented before. It is more important that the information you collect be true and complete and that your presentation of it put it in a new perspective than that you have made a futile effort of doggedly going over vast amounts of information only tangentially related to your subject. One test of the researcher is how well he exercises his judgment in determining what is important for his work and what is not.

Unlike Wordsworth, some topics offer little or no choice of bibliographical tools. Before 1968 there was no bibliography for English stylistics. In the case of no bibliography at all, the researcher can only follow the leads he finds in his core material and use his wit and intuition to discover other relevant material. On obscure subjects which have been little studied, it may be feasible to collect a comprehensive bibliography and read all the material in it. The *PMLA* bibliographies, supplemented before 1956 by other annual bibliographies, would yield most of what had been written in scholarly journals about a very minor literary figure. The topic with an ideally limited bibliography, however, may have other flaws, such as dullness. Not only each field, but each topic, has its own bibliographic problems, and the solution of those problems is part of the researcher's task.

You need to remind yourself, too, that current bibliographies lag behind what is already printed and available. To catch up on the most current publications you must depend on your imagination and the familiarity with your field you have acquired. All books appearing in the catalogs of most publishers are included in the *Publishers' Trade List Annual*, which is indexed by author and title in *Books in Print: An Author-Title-Series Index to "The Publishers' Trade List Annual,"* 2 v. (New York, R.R. Bowker, 1874-date), and by subject in *Subject Guide to Books in Print: An Index to "The Publishers' Trade List Annual,"* 2 v. (New York: R.R. Bowker. 1957-date.) You can also check the tables of contents of periodicals which you know publish work on your subject.

In addition to the authors and titles of published works, the person undertaking a long-term, probably book-length project may find a list of works in progress. No research project should be abandoned, however, because something similar appears on such a list. Projects are sometimes abandoned, and often two researchers approach the same subject from perspectives so different that both make genuine contributions. Should you discover that someone else is working on the subject of your thesis, you can write to him inquiring about his approach and progress. It is entirely possible that an exchange of information would be beneficial to both projects.

THE CARD CATALOG

Once you have a clear idea of what material you are looking for in the library, the next job is extracting it from the stacks and other sources. The usual place to begin is the card catalog, which will normally contain for every book an author card, a title card, and at least one subject card. These cards may be interfiled into a single catalog, or one catalog may contain cards for authors and titles and a second subject cards. A separate catalog or list is sometimes maintained for periodicals. The cards themselves will probably be Library of Congress cards or cards that closely follow the Library of Congress format. Here is an example of a Library of Congress card:

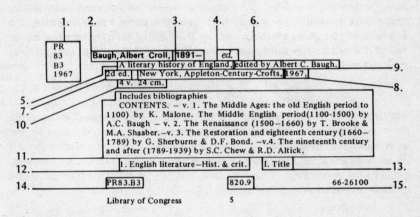

1. The call number for the book in this library.
2. The name of the person or institution responsible for the book — the author or compiler.
3. His birth date and, if he has died, his death date.
4. His role if he is not the author.
5. Title of the work.
6. The author, editor, or compiler's role as given on the title page of the book.
7. Edition number if other than first.
8. Place of publication and publisher.
9. Date of publication. Brackets indicate that the information was not on the title page. Here 1967 is the copyright date taken from the reverse side of the title page.
10. The number of pages or volumes in the work and the height of the book.
11. Information about the contents of the book.
12. Arabic numerals indicate Library of Congress subject classifications. In this case there is only one.
13. Roman numerals indicate additional cards printed for the author and title catalog. In addition to the card to be filed for the title, cards might be printed for a second author or a series title.
14. Library of Congress call number.
15. Dewey Decimal Classification number. In a large library using the Dewey Decimal system an additional number, the Cutter number, would be added.

Of course, the call number in the upper left hand corner, in this case a Library of Congress number, tells you where the book is located and enables you to go to the stacks to get it yourself or to call it from the shelves if the stacks are closed to the public. The card gives other information which may be useful. For example, it gives the complete name of the author and his dates, information that is useful in cases where two authors have similar names. For example, several authors have the name Paul Goodman; the middle name separates the books of one from the books of another, and even though the reader may not know the middle name of the author he is seeking, the dates and subjects of the books together provide telling clues.

The card also gives the publisher and date of publication, which provide some evidence about whether or not a book will be useful. For example, if a scholarly book is privately printed, the author may have paid to have the book published because no commercial or scholarly publisher thought the book worthy of publication. Moreover, in some subjects information rapidly becomes obsolete. If a researcher is interested in the most recent information, the date of publication tells him how old the material had to be to be included in the book.

The card also gives the number of pages or volumes and their size. From the sample card we can see that this particular literary history contains four volumes, and we can, therefore, expect substantial coverage. The title of the fourth volume indicates that the history stops at 1939. Thus, although we can hope the discussion of the periods covered will be updated to approximately the date of publication of the second edition, 1967, we can eliminate this history if we are interested in English literary history after World War II. The card also indicates that bibliographies are included (actually the bibliographical information is contained in footnotes), so that while we might not expect to find extensive coverage of any one literary figure, the bibliographical information could provide useful leads.

Finally, the card indicates what other cards there are for the book, in particular the subject heading that the Library of Congress chose for the book. Thus, if you know of one book on your subject, the catalog card for that book would indicate the subject heading for other books on the same subject. Notice that the sample book has only one subject heading which is quite broad. Despite the lengthy treatment of Middle English literature, no subject card would lead you to it, an example of the trend to fewer subject cards for books. The trend assumes the library user will explore the printed bibliographical sources of the reference room.

Using a card catalog effectively requires knowledge of the finer points of the library's system of alphabetizing. The larger the library, the more important this is, and in a large library with an interfiled subject and author catalog, it is imperative. Common problems include:

Does the library alphabetize letter by letter or word by word? In a letter by letter system word boundaries are ignored, so that "classic*al* antiquities" would come before "classic *scul*pture." In a word by word system, all entries with the same word are filed together, and, therefore, "classic sculpture" would come before "classical antiquities."

How does the library file German Ö? Often this is filed under oe. In general, when a diacritical mark appears in a foreign name or word, you need to know what the diacritical mark means and how it is alphabetized by the library.

Where does the library file M', Mc, and Mac? Often these are interfiled together at the beginning of M. How are the subtopics of a subject ordered? And how are subject cards ordered in relation to authors who may also be subjects?

After you find an appropriate card in the catalog, you need to be able to interpret any code marks the library uses. Your library may have a system of marking a card when a book is temporarily removed from the general collection and placed somewhere like the reserve room. The key which deciphers red lines, blue dots, and other code marks is usually posted near the catalog. If when you find an appropriate card you record the call number directly on your bibliography card, you should never have to consult the catalog again for that particular book.

LIBRARY STACKS

Libraries with closed stacks have the reader fill out a call slip with the catalog number and, usually, the author and title of the book. Although closed stacks mean that you will not be able to browse through the books, you have at least the consolation that fewer books are misplaced, lost, or stolen from closed stacks than from open stacks. If you keep a record of the books you called from the stacks, you will know which books are not brought to you, and if neither the book nor the call clip is returned, you can assume that the first call slip was lost and submit another.

If the stacks are open, you can browse among the books near the ones you have found to see if there are others which might be useful. The price you pay for this privilege is having to find the books yourself. The better you know your library, the more of your books you will find. Some libraries, for example, store books that are too large for the regular shelves on a separate set of shelves for oversize books. That the book is oversize may not be indicated on the catalog card or in the number, so the reader must remember to check the oversize shelf. Also, books that have been returned by previous readers are usually sorted in some preliminary fashion and stored in a place convenient to the stack area where they are to be replaced. Knowing where these areas are provides another place to check if the book is not on the shelf.

Some libraries which have outgrown their present facilities store little-used books in another building known as the annex. If your book, or more likely periodical, is not on the shelf and is either old or esoteric, a check of the shelf list should indicate if it has been moved from the stacks. The shelf list is a catalog in which a card for each book is filed according to catalog number. Often the shelf list card is the most carefully maintained for changes in location, and the shelf list card may contain the most accurate record of holdings for periodicals.

If you fail to find a book, usually the clerk at the circulation desk can tell you if it has been checked out, and, if it has, you may request the book be held for you when it is returned or even have it called back to the library for your use. If the book is not checked out, and if your own detective work fails, then you can ask to have the book traced. It is, however, usually faster to do as much of the tracing as possible yourself.

INTERLIBRARY LOAN

To use a book or periodical which your library does not own you can buy it if it is still in print, have your library borrow it from another on interlibrary loan, or go to another library and use the book there. Since the General Interlibrary Loan Code of 1952 specifies certain materials which should not be requested by interlibrary loan, including current issues of periodicals and items which are in print and can be bought inexpensively, a check of *Books in Print* may make the choice for you. In addition, libraries may not request a large number of books for a single borrower, for the borrower's library or the borrower himself is expected to buy the bulk of material needed for a major research project. Moreover, libraries are naturally reluctant to send out rare and valuable material.

The request form for interlibrary loan asks for two bibliographical sources for the book. The first would be the book or bibliography in which you found the reference. The second, which verifies the existence of the book or article and the accuracy of the citation, can be found in another bibliography. For a book, one obvious source for the second reference is the appropriate catalog of cards printed by the Library of Congress.

Rather than lending a periodical, libraries prefer to photocopy the relevant article, and if you know what part of a book you want, and if copying that section is not construed to be a violation of copyright by the lending library, portions of books will be photocopied in preference to loaning the book. Thus, complete accurate bibliographical information is essential. Convenience as well as the restrictions of the Interlibrary Loan Code discourages heavy dependence on the procedure, for it can take several weeks for the book to arrive. Finally, you may be asked to pay a fee for interlibrary loan, the amount of which may be unknown in advance and which can be quite high.

An alternative to interlibrary loan is to organize your research so that you can go to a larger library if there is one close enough to make such a trip feasible. To do this you would want to have references for enough sources to make the pilgrimage worthwhile, enough so that if one book or periodical were missing you could look at other sources instead. Also, it is wise before you make such a trip to inquire into the library's policy concerning "visiting scholars," for you may need a letter of introduction from another librarian, a dean, or a similar authority to use the library.

EVALUATING SOURCES

As you acquire relevant books and articles you begin extensive reading and note-taking, although you may have taken some notes during your preliminary reading. During your research you will probably examine both primary and secondary sources. A primary source can be an eyewitness account in a newspaper, diary, or letter; a poem or novel if the paper involves literary study; an historical document; census data; the raw data from a sociological survey; or the uninterpreted results of a scientific experiment. A secondary source is an interpretation, paraphrase or analysis by a student, scholar, or researcher using primary sources. Some secondary sources are secondary in name only and are really much farther removed from the primary material. You must appraise how close the author of a secondary source is to primary sources because you must evaluate all your sources. Primary sources, of course, can be as misleading as secondary sources. The letters of a known braggart or the explanation of someone deeply implicated in an incident which he would want interpreted in a certain way must be regarded with at least as much scepticism as a scholar's analysis of an event or circumstance. The conscientious researcher must weigh the analysis or interpretation of a secondary source against primary source material even when everyone seems to agree.

An example is the long-held notion that the bawdy stories which belong to the medieval genre of the fabliau were bourgeois or lower-class in their orientation and origin. The incongruous picture of the decorous audience of noblemen and noblewomen who listened to tales of courtesy and chivalry also listening to stories and poems much more scatological and sexually explicit than anything in Chaucer led generations of scholars to accept the nineteenth-century thesis that two classes of literature appealed to two social classes. In such a system the fabliau definitely belongs to the bourgeois class. But a Danish scholar, Per Nykrog, went back to the fabliaux and did a systematic study of the literary themes and conventions as well as of the manuscripts in which the fabliaux were recorded, and he found compelling evidence of the appeal of some fabliaux to an aristocratic audience familiar with chivalric and courtly literature. The citation of conventions found in fabliaux and the description of physical evidence in the manuscripts are examples of dependence on primary sources. To cite Nykrog or a different scholar who argues for a bourgeois audience would be using a secondary source in a discussion of fabliaux, but a primary source in a discussion of current arguments about the fabliau.

No adequate research paper relies on secondary sources alone, but a solid research paper is likely to rely very little on secondary sources. Of course the use of previous analysis and interpretation is not a bad thing in itself, for knowledge will not advance if we are not willing to build on the work of others, but secondary sources must be evaluated by the scope and use they make of their primary sources and the findings of one secondary source must be weighed against the findings of others concerned with the same facts or data.

TAKING NOTES

In your reading and note-taking, then, you are at least as concerned with the arguments and evidence a scholar uses to support his statements and the assumptions which underlie his interpretations as you are with the statements and interpretations themselves, and the notes you take should enable you to recall the arguments and assumptions readily. Of course you cannot prove every statement you make, and knowledge advances because scholars and researchers agree to accept certain facts, yet you should be prepared to defend the assumptions you do accept. The quality of your examination of the previous scholarship will weigh heavily in the evaluation of your work by your instructor, director, or peers. Hence note-taking must be an analytical procedure in which you record your ideas and your perceptions of primary and secondary sources.

Because note-taking is analytical rather than mechanical, a photocopy is not a note. Although photocopies cannot serve as notes, they are useful. If you are going to be conscientious about verifying every quotation and citation in the final draft, there are enormous advantages to buying the most pertinent books and photocopying the most significant passages from books and articles that you don't own, especially if your project is long. In all probability, some of your material will have to stay in the library, and if your research goes on over several months, or even years, the librarians may demand you return circulating books before the end of the project. Having photocopies at hand means that you won't have to go back to the stacks or recall volumes you have already checked out once before. But however useful, a collection of photocopies is no substitute for a collection of notes.

A note, then, is a record, most often of ideas, but it may on rare occasions simply record a bare fact, such as "In Utah in 1968 a condemned man selected either hanging or shooting as the method of execution." A note may record a summary of an article which interprets a small number of facts in a relatively simple way. For example:

John E. Williams and John R. Stables in "If White Means Good Then Black . . ." (*Psychology Today*, 7 (July, 1973), 51-54) cite numerous experiments that show that pre-schoolers have already acquired negative associations with the color black and positive associations with the color white. These associations are found in many cultures, and studies have shown some connection between the strength of such association and racial bias. Therefore, the authors suggest that terms such as Euro-American be used instead of the names of colors to distinguish among races.

Such a summary does not include everything in the article. For example, the authors also describe an educational program which seems to reduce racial prejudice in young children, and they cite some experiments which tested th. affective value of color names in adolescents and adults. But the summary does capture the elements emphasized in the article — the response of small children and the authors' concern about the use of color terms for racial distinctions.

A note may paraphrase or summarize a paragraph from a book or article instead of attempting to summarize the whole work, especially if the work is complex or if only a portion of it is relevant to the writer's project. For example, here is a paragraph from Arthur R. Miller's *The Assault on Privacy: Computers, Data Banks, and Dossiers* (Ann Arbor: The University of Michigan Press, 1971):

> Some blacks have argued that many census questions have racial overtones and are designed to identify the black community for possible separation from the larger population should a crisis arise. They see the census as working hand in glove with such legislative proposals as those involving stop and frisk, preventive detention, the establishment of incarceration camps for use during civil disturbances, as well as with what many believe is the white establishment's conspiracy to exterminate black militants. Despite reasoned defenses against these attacks, the government's credibility gap seems too wide for many blacks to bridge. (p. 148)

The paragraph might be paraphrased in this way:

> Blacks who have been sensitized by legislation apparently aimed at them, e.g. stop and frisk, preventive detention, and proposed detention facilities for demonstrators and rioters, resent census questions which they believe could be used to identify and locate them in times of critical racial tension.

The paragraph might be summarized thus:

> Some blacks are hostile to the census because they believe some questions have racial overtones and because they fear the government could use the information to harass or incarcerate them.

Finally, a note may be the simple transcription of a direct quotation. Such notes should be kept to a minimum. If note-taking is to be efficient, you must have a clear enough conception of your subject to separate the relevant fact or opinion from its context when you are doing extensive reading. In the example above, unless the specific legislative proposals which have aroused black distrust are relevant to the topic of the paper, they can be left out. By carefully focusing the note, you save time not only in writing the note out but also in reading and weeding your notes when you are composing your report. Simply transcribing a direct quotation is a mechanical, time-consuming procedure which does none of the intellectual sorting out required to write the report. It is a step to be eliminated whenever possible.

Direct quotations are called for when an author's statement is so striking and concise that it deserves to be reproduced verbatim, or when it could be rephrased only at much greater length. A direct quotation may be necessary if you are going to discuss, analyze, or take issue with it. And a direct quotation might be used to prove that what has been held to be the opinion of its author is inaccurate or even contrary to what he is saying in the passage being quoted. Ideally, in your note-taking, however, you will routinely try to summarize first, then paraphrase, and then, after a conscious decision about the purpose of the quotation, quote verbatim.

The form of a note must include certain features. It must be legible and permanent; hence the frequent recommendation of pen over pencil. It is wise to limit yourself to one vehicle, always using a 4 x 6 inch card or 11 x 8½ inch sheet of paper or whatever suits you. It is bad policy to keep a note on the back of a menu, not because the menu will not fit tidily into a pack of note cards, but because a week later you may well forget the note and discard the menu. Likewise any odd group of notes is too easily set aside and forgotten. The nature of the material you are working with in your research and your own inclinations will determine whether you use notecards, notebooks, or some sort of loose leaf arrangement.

Whatever arrangement you choose, however, if you always use only one side of a card or sheet, you will not lose a note on the reverse side. Whether you use cards or paper, leave some blank space for your comments at a later date. When you take the note you can indicate somewhere the special aspect of your topic with which your note deals, but the extra space allows for changes in that concept as well as other comments such as, "but see Smith on the use of census figures for social planning," or "see also Jones's comment," or "number inconsistent with estimate of Arbuthnot."

Finally, whatever form your note takes, it must include a record of the source such that if you found the note two months later under your desk and isolated from all your other notes, you could go directly to the page of the book or article from which it came. This can be done in the same form a footnote would take in the final draft, or in a shortened footnote form including the author's name, a shortened title, and the page, or even more briefly by some code keyed to your bibliography cards plus the page number. The first pattern is the most tedious and least risky, the last is the fastest and most fraught with danger. If you omit this information, you virtually guarantee having to go back through at least some of your sources to find the origin of a quotation, fact, or opinion that was left partially or wholly unidentified.

In addition to noting facts, interpretations, and opinions, you may also want to note discrepancies you discover and questions that occur to you as you read. If you keep a separate sheet or notebook for such discoveries and thoughts, you can make a quick note and continue your reading. Later you will have a collection of questions and facts that need further research, and you can organize them for efficient use of the library.

PRELIMINARY WRITING

In the hierarchy between the note and first draft may come a written preliminary analysis of a literary work, an argument, or an experiment. If you are working with a project which permits early acquisition of the source material which you are going to interpret in some way, you can write a preliminary interpretation. This exercise can point out those areas which need the most attention before the work can be finished and also those relatively elementary questions which can be solved quickly, sometimes adding a significant insight. For example, if your project includes interpreting a number of poems, the effort you put into an early analysis may point to simple trouble spots — a word, for example, that is used ambiguously, or an inverted grammatical structure which emphasizes a statement, or alerts you to a previously unperceived aspect of an image. Such preliminary writing can clarify your own perceptions and ideas, point to new directions for your research, and give you practice in writing about the subject. Such practice may, in turn, speed the first draft by providing usable passages and increasing self assurance with writing about the topic. Thus the effort put into preliminary writing can save time by focusing research and by cutting the effort needed to produce the first draft.

WRITING HABITS

Writing is difficult at best, and to write well consistently requires discipline. A look into the studies of professional writers shows that most have a routine they follow for writing. Hemingway, for example, wrote every morning. A routine time may be supported by rituals, as in the case of Nabokov, who composes in longhand standing at a lectern. Such routines and rituals have value because they establish writing as a habit in certain circumstances. Thus, anyone who has to write an extensive report or many short reports needs to set aside a time and a place for writing and to accustom himself to writing there and then.

The skill involved in writing is not unlike other skills: it atrophies with lack of use. If when you sit down to write your first draft you have not written for some time, you can expect to have a slow, jerky beginning. Likewise, unless you have become accustomed to writing for long stretches at a time, you probably should not plan on working for more than about three hours at a sitting. For virtually everyone, three hours a day for five consecutive days will prove more productive than fifteen hours crammed into one or two days, especially for someone who has done no writing at all for a while. Although the writing itself will never become routine, you can establish a writing time and a writing ritual. Do you work best composing at a typewriter? Are you more comfortable writing in longhand? Know what you need at hand to write comfortably, have it available, and then sit down and write.

If you have not developed writing habits yet, and if you can type, learning to compose at the typewriter has two advantages. First, your manuscript will always be legible, even to a typist who doesn't know you. Second, once you are used to the typewriter, you will type faster than you can write in longhand and thus be able to record ideas faster.

THE FIRST DRAFT

The poet's advice was to look in your heart and write, but the researcher generally begins by looking at his notes. If your notes are in fact notes and not a collection of quotations, you will avoid the first trap in the way of the writer — the temptation to string together a series of quotations on a slender wisp of tedious, predictable prose. The next temptation, one that has been too often encouraged, is to think that to give your material shape you need merely order your notes and string them together with a similar wisp of transitional remarks. Writing is harder work than that.

You will, of course, before you begin writing the first draft, review your notes and sort them according to the topics which emerge as important and related. If you can possibly put your notes aside and then write, letting your mind select the emphasis and give the material the shape that you are creating for it, your first draft should emerge the honest work of your mind. If you keep your notes at your side instead of simply referring to them to confirm points and check facts, you may unwittingly let them dampen or control your own intellectual processes.

Before you write you will also have made some decisions about the structure of your paper and the elements you want emphasized. The point that you are making should help to determine how it is presented, even though some topics lend themselves to a particular format. Biography, for example, is often presented chronologically, but a biography of Noam Chomsky might reasonably begin with a description of his antiwar activism, and then show how his background led to his study of linguistics as an attack on the structure of the social sciences, thus showing that his work in linguistics is actually based on the same concerns as his political writing and action. That many dissertations and scholarly articles begin with a review of the research does not mean they all have to, or even that some wouldn't have been improved by a less conventional beginning.

If you can construct an outline before you write, and if you find such an outline useful, then make an outline. But despite frequent pedagogical imperatives on the subject, many successful writers do not begin with outlines. If you find an outline constraining or if you find one tedious to construct, don't bother. If you need an outline to go with the paper, you can outline it after it is written. No one consciously parses a sentence before he speaks it, and just as you must have the sentence to parse it, you must have worked out the structure of the paper to outline it. Some people, of course, do work out the structure sufficiently in advance to construct detailed outlines — a room in Faulkner's house is papered with the working outlines of the chapters of one of his novels. Other people prefer working from a simple list of major topics or ideas.

Reports usually follow one of two patterns. In the first, a conclusion is presented and argued for. In the second, a question or problem is presented followed by pertinent data and one or several hypotheses which explain it. If several hypotheses are presented, they are tested or evaluated to demonstrate which are most satisfactory. Although the second pattern appears to represent the actual course of the researcher's work, it is a much simplified representation, for no one wants to read about every mistake made and tangent taken by the writer in the course of his work.

In addition to deciding on a general scheme for the paper, you need to decide exactly what audience you are writing for. A college or university student can assume that he is writing for his classmates. The term paper submitted at the end of American History I is usually addressed to an audience with the preparation for the course even though the only reader may be an instructor who knows much more about American History. Similarly, papers for an advanced seminar, which are often formally exchanged during the term, are addressed to students ready for the advanced work. In the case of a thesis or dissertation, the writer can reasonably assume an audience of scholars in his general field, but not specialists on his particular topic. Anyone on the faculty in the student's department should be comfortable reading the paper. The dissertation writer has become a specialist in his field, and he is writing for intelligent, informed non-specialists.

Having reviewed your notes, selected the general method of presentation and points for emphasis, and reminded yourself of the needs of the audience, begin to write, but not necessarily at the beginning. A systematic person who normally begins at the beginning will probably do so. But if you are less systematic, and you are particularly confident or excited about one particular topic, begin with that, especially since first paragraphs and first chapters are among the most difficult to write. Wherever you begin, you may find your early paragraphs unsatisfactory, but instead of going back to rewrite them, forge ahead. With any luck at all, as you get into writing your ideas will begin to flow and the words will begin to flow with them. Since you will not want to do anything to discourage this, do not stop to look up words in the dictionary, to check a fact, or to go into the next room for a book. Instead of worrying about the antecedents of pronouns, lack of parallelism, or even prepositions at the ends of sentences, work to maintain the momentum of your writing, a momentum highly vulnerable to interruption. You will, of course, want to be coherent and convincing, so you cannot simply proceed on the basis of free association of ideas, but in the first draft two crudely stated ideas are more valuable than one elegantly stated.

If the momentum of your writing stops, simply rereading what you have written may help you regain it. Sometimes you will find that you are trying to trace several different but related arguments or lines of development at the same time. Often a writer begins with one line of development, some aspect of which is linked to the second, and he is sidetracked to the second before finishing the first. If this has interrupted your progress, try to set aside the sections on the peripheral argument, go back to developing the first, and then plan to follow up on second and even third strands at other points.

As you work on an extended project, or as you complete several small projects, you will develop a sense of about how much you can expect of yourself at a sitting. Although some sessions will go better than others, and although if you expect to do much research writing you will try to extend your limits, it is dangerous to try to push too far beyond them. For most people it is better to stop with a few good ideas left, jot them down, and then pick them up at the next session. Then the writer has a running start when he sits down to continue his work.

Even after you have finished your major reading and note-taking, you may find your conception of your subject changing. Such a change can happen even while you are writing. In *Crisis in the Classroom: The Remaking of American Education* (1970; reprinted New York: Vintage, 1971) Charles E. Silberman describes some of the changes that this particular research report, researched and written by a professional, went through. He says of his book:

> . . . the question of purpose kept intruding itself throughout the course of the research, and even more, through the course of writing. Writing is always painful, for it is a continuous process of dialogue with oneself, of confrontation with one's thoughts, ideas, and feelings.
>
> . . . .
>
> It was not until I was well into the writing, therefore — not until I had, over a summer, completed and abandoned a first crude draft — that I began to realize what a metamorphosis had taken place in me and in my thinking about education. In struggling to find my theme, I discovered that my views had changed profoundly. I had not thought hard enough about educational purpose until the agony of writing forced me to; I thought I *knew* what the purpose of education should be: namely, intellectual development.
>
> . . . .
>
> I was wrong. (pp 6-7)

Silberman was a senior editor *of Fortune*, a researcher and writer of experience and proven talent, when he undertook the Carnegie Study of Education and Educators which led to the book. His description of the act of composition ill accords with the portrait of the unruffled student writing sedately at a desk with his detailed outline, in perfect parallel form, at one side, his notes at the other, casually knocking out his term paper. Unfortunately that portrait has often been seriously offered to students as a model for their own work. In contrast, Silberman testifies that writing is not easy, but agony. He found he needed not to revise his first draft, but to abandon it and start over. For that to happen to a student is not evidence of his incompetence and inefficiency. Instead it may witness to his intellectual honesty.

Earlier in the introduction Silberman talks about the mysterious process of change by which books become something other than what they start out to be (p. 3). The internal dialogue which ultimately defines the topic and shapes the paper is the product of the individual researcher's mind coming to grips with the material his research has provided. There is no guide through those dark woods. One can only suggest you keep at the dialogue, that is, keep on writing, until the conversation with yourself reaches a natural, satisfactory end. Then you will have a draft which represents a statement of your work, a draft which you can begin to revise and refine. Such revision is basic to the intellectual quality of the paper, for since — as Northrop Frye has said — "the words used are the form of which ideas are the content," a crudely stated idea is, in fact, a crude idea.

REVISION

Like crudities in our children, crudities in our writing are often difficult to perceive, and the critical objectivity necessary to see them accumulates with time. Ideally the first draft is set aside for several days before revision begins. If several days are out of the question, at least allow several hours of rest and diversion before tackling the revision. Because large important changes should be made first, revision begins with the questions of how convincing is the argument and how well proportioned are the treatments of various subtopics. You may discover you could improve your argument by rearranging the subsections of the paper or that you could significantly cut a section which you found particularly interesting but does not deserve the prominence of your extended treatment. You may find, too, that you have assumed too much knowledge of certain aspects and therefore need to add explanatory sentences or paragraphs. Such large revisions are common to all reports, but since their specific character is determined by the individual report and author, there are no general rules for guidance. Such changes can be made conveniently, however, only if you have allowed plenty of space on the pages of the first draft, double or triple space on a typewriter with wide margins, and if you have written on one side of the sheet only. Cutting and pasting will not solve all your problems, but it can help solve some, and it is impossible if both sides of the sheet have been used.

TRANSITIONS

Although such evaluation of argument, evidence, and proportion is unique to each project, other problems of research writing are widely shared, and can be described more specifically. Transitions, for example, are essential for clarity; indeed, they are at the very heart of your research, for they show how you perceived some new idea, concept, or likeness which put your disparate data into an organized framework. Perception of the whole is only part of the job; you have to make that perception obvious to your reader, and you can do that only through the transitional devices you use among sentences, paragraphs, and topics.

The transitional problems of the paragraphs are similar to those of the larger report. Just as there is no set formula for a research report, there is no set formula for a paragraph. Indeed, it is hard to imagine anything more tedious than a series of paragraphs all constructed on the model of topic sentence — amplification — restatement. Nevertheless, the reader is entitled to an orderly progression of thought which is simple, clear, and direct. That is where transitions guide him from point to point. Thus you must provide early in the paragraph a link to what has gone before, and you must provide links among the rest of the sentences of the paragraph. It is not sufficient that the facts or ideas are related in your intellectual apprehension of the subject, for that apprehension must be made immediate to the reader. Here are five stylistic devices which accomplish this:

1. Maintaining the same grammatical subject in a series of sentences.
2. Using complex sentences which, by virtue of the fact of grammatical subordination, make relationships among the parts clear.
3. Repetition of key words, as opposed to elegant variation.
4. Parallelism
5. Using adverbs which express relationships, such as *moreover, therefore, nevertheless,* and *for example.*

Here is a paragraph from Muriel Beadle's *A Child's Mind: How Children Learn During the Critical Years from Birth to Age Five* (1970, rpt. Garden City, New York: Anchor Books, 1971):

As the varying cultural patterns of the world's peoples attest, young humans are enormously adaptable, and older humans are exceptionally faithful to the ways of their forebears. A baby can learn to sleep upright and tightly swaddled, or prone and without a cover. If his mother elects not to carry him in a sling on her back during the day and keep him in her bed at night, he adjusts very well to spending long solitary periods in his crib or playpen. As a newborn, he feeds whenever he is hungry or according to some externally imposed schedule, and grows into a pattern of eating once a day or five times a day — not because such behavior is best in any absolute sense but because it is customary in his culture. (pp. 218-19)

This typical paragraph from a sound, readable book provides several examples of transitional devices. The words "cultural patterns" in the first sentence refer back to the subject of the previous paragraph, thus linking the two paragraphs. The first sentence is complex, the dependent clause containing the link to what has gone before, and the first independent clause, "young humans are enormously adaptable," is the general statement which is amplified by the rest of the paragraph. All of the examples given in the paragraph show the adaptation as a response to the demands of "older humans," the grammatical subject of the second independent clause of the first sentence. "Young humans" is made more specific in "a baby" in the second sentence, and "a baby," through the pronoun *he*, remains the grammatical subject of the rest of the sentences in the paragraph. The last clause, "not because such behavior is best in any absolute sense but because it is customary in his culture" anticipates the following paragraph which discusses the effect of culture on values and habits which may be seen as absolute by the reader, a view which the author challenges.

While we do not know what changes the paragraph went through in the actual writing, we can imagine how it would look with less care for such verbal clarity:

People are highly adaptable to the patterns of their forebears, and they perpetuate those patterns. Some babies learn to sleep tightly swaddled in an upright position. In some societies infants are left without a blanket lying down. There are mothers who carry their babies with them in slings and even sleep with them in their bed. Young children elsewhere are content to play by themselves in cribs or playpens. There are cultures in which mothers feed their babies according to a fixed schedule. Other children are allowed to nurse when they are hungry. Such patterns are not adapted to by the child because they are good or bad intrinsically, but because they are imposed by the culture.

This version is inferior because it is a succession of loose and unrelated sentences. Instead of setting cultural contrasts in opposition in the same sentence, the contrasts are stated in separate sentences with emphasis shifting with grammatical subject from mother to child to culture. This constant, unnecessary shifting of grammatical subjects makes the paragraph harder to follow and the pronoun references confusing even though they are grammatically correct. Moreover, the hierarchy in importance for this paragraph of culture, parent, and child is less clearly defined. Thus, in the original, the careful provision of transitional devices creates greater clarity by indicating what is more and less important and by focusing on the subject.

Just as relationships among the sentences of a paragraph need to be presented to the reader unambiguously, so too do the relationships of topic to topic. Depending on the work and the author, such relationships may be indicated simply or may demand extensive statement.

For example, chapter six, "Earth's Green Mantle," of Rachel Carson's *Silent Spring* (Boston: Houghton Mifflin, 1962) begins, "Water, soil, and the earth's green mantle of plants make up the world that supports the animal life of the earth." (p. 63). The first two words, "water" and "soil," refer to the subjects of chapters four and five.

Similarly, Konrad Lorenz restates the subject of the previous chapter at the beginning of chapter five of *On Aggression*, trans. Marjorie Kerr Wilson (New York: Harcourt Brace & World, 1966), but Lorenz explicitly states the relationship of the previous topic to the new one:

> Redirection of the attack is evolution's most ingenious expedient for guiding aggression into harmless channels, and it is not the only one, for rarely do the great constructors, selection and mutation, rely on a *single* method. It is the nature of their blind trial and error, or to be more exact, trial and success, that they often hit upon *several* possible ways of dealing with the same problem, and use them all to make its solution doubly and triply sure. (p. 57)

In this case, "redirection of the attack" has been the subject of the previous chapter, and this chapter will go on to discuss three more mechanisms for channeling aggression in animals which are paralleled in man.

Even more explicit is Jean Piaget's beginning paragraph of chapter three of *The Language and Thought of the Child*, trans. Marjorie and Ruth Gabain, 3rd ed., International Library of Psychology, Philosophy and Scientific Method (London: Routledge & Kegan Paul Ltd., 1959):

> In the preceding chapters we have tried to determine to what extent children speak to each other and think socially. An essential problem has been left on one side: when children talk together, do they understand one another? This is the problem which we are now to discuss. (p. 76)

Another example, this time making use of summary and enumeration, comes from chapter four of G.R. Owst's *Literature and Pulpit in Medieval England: A Neglected Chapter in the History of English Letters & of the History of the English People* (Cambridge: Cambridge University Press, 1933):

> Three distinctive types of medieval sermon-illustrations have already been noticed and discussed, more especially from the point of view of their literary influence, in the chapters preceding. We have seen brief

illustrations drawn from men and things in the current everyday scene. We have had examples of the allegorical *figure* of speech, often Scriptural in origin but non-scriptural in its development; and in addition we have had occasion to observe the part played by Biblical hero and saint in the pulpit legend. There remains yet the commonest type of *exemplum* to be considered, the moralized anecdote, whether historically true or fictitious, drawn from sources both ancient and contemporary, secular as well as religious (p. 149).

Owst goes on in the paragraph to indicate the literary importance of the sermon *exemplum* and to explain why his discussion will emphasize how *exampla* were disseminated in England.

Summaries such as this which are used in transitions to move the reader from one topic to another are not superfluous. Rather than clogging the report with boring repetition they ease the reader from one section to another smoothly and thus support the structure of the paper.

DOCUMENTATION AND CITATION

The need for transitions is matched only by the need for evidence. Indeed, although it is possible to provide too much, it is most difficult, especially if the evidence is not presented in a clearly organized and rational way. The facts and interpretations you have uncovered in your research are equivalent to the individualizing detail of the novel. Without them there is no life in the work. While you do not want to simply string together a series of quotations or paraphrases, you will need to document facts, and you may want to cite the opinions of others. Both can be done gracefully and must be done accurately.

The Muriel Beadle paragraph quoted assumed that some of the wide cultural differences in child rearing were common knowledge. Since most readers will be aware that in some societies children are carried in slings while their mothers work in the fields and in other societies children are left in their cribs while their mothers vacuum the house, a footnote to an anthropological study independently verifying such observations is unnecessary. But one must document more esoteric facts, or ones which the reader might challenge. For example, in *Fire in the Lake: The Vietnamese and the Americans in Vietnam* (Boston: Little, Brown, 1972) Frances Fitzgerald footnotes the statement, "By 1959 South Vietnam was importing twenty million dollars worth of food per year under the Food for Peace Plan though food was still its greatest national resource" (p. 102). The note in this case directs the reader to Bernard B. Fall's *The Two Vietnams: A Political and Military Analysis* (New York: Praeger, 1963), pp. 294-295. Such a note serves two purposes. First, it acknowledges the source where the author found her information, and second, it enables the reader to go to that source to evaluate it for himself and check whether the author has quoted accurately and with due respect for the context.

Just as you provide the source for facts, so you provide the source for interpretations and opinions. Even when you have reexamined the evidence and independently reached a conclusion, if that conclusion has already been stated by someone else, the other author must be clearly acknowledged in the paper. Whether you agree or not, the text of your paper must show just where the interpretation begins and ends with a minimum of fuss and footnotes.

In a paraphrase, the simplest way is to begin with the name of the author as Jessie Bernard does here in a paragraph from *Academic Women* (University Park: The Pennsylvania State University Press, 1964):

> Caplow and McGee report that the evaluation of professors as men-of-knowledge is more difficult in some areas than in others, most difficult in the "feminine" subjects like English and least so in the "masculine" subjects like physics. They found the difficulty of evaluation in the social sciences to lie between the complexity of the humanities and the relative simplicity of the physical sciences. Whether any specific categorization or classification of academic men in terms of content of their contribution, method, or political stance was considered good or bad, they found, depended, of course, on the evaluator. In any event, they concluded, it was based on "performance and is as equitable as conflicts of viewpoint permit." (p. 139)

Because the paragraph opens with the names of the authors of the original work, and since it is clear that only one work is under discussion, the footnote can be reserved for the end of the paragraph, which because it ends with a direct quotation must be documented precisely. Jessie Bernard is here showing her scepticism of the objectivity possible in evaluating professors as men-of-knowledge by pointing to inconsistencies in Caplow and McGee, and, in turn, her scepticism gives greater force to her subsequent quotation of the authors to the effect that women professors are not evaluated as men-of-knowledge at all. Thus, she is quoting for a purpose.

The facts and opinions you document in your paper should be there either to be refuted, or to buttress your own argument or interpretation.

Simple agreement with a previous analysis is seldom worthy of inclusion. To say, "I agree with John Doe who argues that a free press is valuable," with or without either a summary of John Doe's opinion or a quotation from his work, is certain to convince the reader that you are simple-minded, unless you go on to show why you agree and what place agreed upon fact or opinion has in the fabric of your argument.

Usually it is graceless to simply pick up a sentence from another author, quote it, and provide only a footnote. Somewhere in the text you need to acknowledge the full measure of your debt to the ideas you found in the work from which the quotation was taken, for normally you would not be quoting from a work which was irrelevant to your argument or which did not help to shape your thought. It is not only graceless but also dishonest to place a mere suspended numeral at the end of a paragraph which summarizes someone else's ideas. You must indicate in the text where the use of someone else's work begins. Hiding his name amidst a sea of closely typed references at the bottom of the page or at the end of the paper is not sufficient acknowledgment. Moreover, your own ideas and work will be more prominent if you are scrupulous about giving due credit to others in the text of your paper. The solution is not more footnotes, but rather a balanced and thorough assessment of your debt to others.

Ideally, then, the text of the research report should be written so that a reader has to consult a footnote which documents a fact or opinion or acknowledges a source only if he (1) wants to learn more about a subject from a source you have cited, (2) wants to check the accuracy of your report, or (3) wants to use the bibliographical information, such as the date of publication, to evaluate the source. The reader should not have to consult the notes, with or without the aid of a ouija board, to determine what is original to the report and what is second hand.

EXPLANATORY FOOTNOTES

A second kind of footnote, the explanatory footnote, is provided when the author wants to include information peripheral to his argument for most of his readers. For example, the Report of the Traffic and Distribution Panel to the Commission on Obscenity and Pornography titles Section D of Part I, "The 'Under-the-Counter' or 'Hard-Core' Pornography Market." The authors note "Hard-Core" and provide the following comments in the note:

Some judges have employed the term "hard-core pornography" as a synonym for "material which can be legally suppressed." In this Report, the term is used as a synonym for "under-the-counter" or covertly sold materials. This is, in effect, the definition of hard-core applied in the marketplace. It can be argued that because of the confusion about the meaning of the term, which stems primarily from an undefined legal concept, it would be well to avoid the use of the term altogether. *(The Report of the Commission on Obscenity and Pornography* (Washington, D.C.: U.S. Government Printing Office, 1970), p. 113).

The note actually restates the definition provided earlier in the text (p. 18) and goes on to defend the report's use of the word to those few in the audience with enough legal experience to know that the word has been used differently in some courts. Clearly, most of the audience of the report would not have that legal experience, and they are free to read the report without attending to the peripheral argument of the footnote. Remember, however, that most academic research reports are addressed to a much narrower audience than that of a report so controversial and publicized that it was commercially reprinted in paperback for newsstand distribution. A careful author can adjust his text to the specific needs of a small audience, and so an academic report normally requires few explanatory footnotes. For those readers who will feel obliged to read all of a report, it is much more convenient to have all of the relevant information incorporated in the text.

STYLE

Although your first concerns in revising the report are for proportion, smooth transitions, and accurate and graceful inclusion of evidence, you will probably make less dramatic changes in syntax and diction while you are attending to the major problems. Often the minor changes will involve little thought or effort, since they consist of eliminating the awkardness characteristic of early drafts. The changes, however, are important to your presentation, for they affect the way the work is received. Naturally, if your contribution is important enough, it will be acknowledged even if the style is off-putting, but it may be acknowledged only grudgingly. Moreover, to be as clear and concise as possible, that is, to write as well as you can, is a courtesy to your reader.

As you refine your presentation, you can apply three tests to the individual sentence and paragraph:
1. Does it say exactly what you mean, no more, no less?
2. Does it say that as concisely as possible?
3. Does it sound good when read aloud?

In addition, you can watch for a number of stylistic mannerisms which are commonly found in academic writing. None of these mannerisms produces ungrammatical sentences, but they clog the prose and diminish the effectiveness of the report. Once you are used to watching for them, eliminating them can be an easy way to improve your writing.

Because the mind can process an active declarative sentence more quickly than a passive sentence, the passive voice is justified only when the agent of the action is unknown or so unimportant that it is better left out. For example, if in the context of the paper it is important that the streets were clear, then

The streets were cleared of snow.

is preferable to

The Department of Streets and Sanitation cleared the streets of snow.

However, when the agent is worthy of inclusion, the active voice is usually preferable, not only because it is more easily absorbed by the reader, but also because the elements of importance receive the natural emphasis given to the first and last places in the sentence.

Thus,

The neighborhood improvement association found property values declining.

avoids the anticlimax of the prepositional phrase at the end of

Property values were found to be declining by the neighborhood improvement association.

Besides changing passives to actives, the emphasis of the final position in a sentence can be used in active sentences by removing modifying phrases from the end:

Experiments have not demonstrated the worth of computers, television, and other educational hardware.

rather than:

Computers, television, and other educational hardware have not proved their worth in the experiments in which they have been tested.

Another device that contributes to clarity and emphasis is parallelism, that is putting similar thoughts in the same grammatical structure, as Lincoln did in the Gettysburg Address:

. . . we cannot dedicate, we cannot consecrate, we cannot hallow this ground.

Surely oblivion would have swallowed up the same thought differently stated:

Mere civilians cannot dedicate this ground. Nor can we consecrate it. It cannot be hallowed either.

Although the simple active declarative sentence can often be emphatic, too many such sentences create boredom. Thus grammatical subordination, which we have seen was valuable in providing transitions by describing relationships of place, time, and cause, also combats monotony. Thus, the following paragraph is both dull and less than fully explanatory:

Jane Austen portrays society in *Emma* as extremely dull. It is a particularly cruel environment for an unmarried woman. The author portrays the society ironically, so we see that Emma is better off married to Mr. Knightley than with any other possible fate.

Grammatical subordination makes the thought clearer and the prose more interesting:

Because the ironically-portrayed society of *Emma* is shown to be particularly cruel to single women, the reader recognizes that Emma is best off married to Mr. Knightley.

Occasionally, however, a complex sentence takes off in several directions at once and becomes confusing:

Because the reader is sympathetic to Emma, who lives in a society which is particularly boring and restricted for the unmarried woman, the reader is happy to see her betrothed to Mr. Knightley, who has proved true to his name and considerate of her father.

Although all of the elements included in the sentence could be important to the interpretation, and although the sentence is grammatically correct, breaking it down into three sentences makes the relationships clearer:

By the end of the novel the reader hopes Emma will not be reduced to the pathetic existence decreed for unmarried women in her society. He also desires a man worthy of her hand, and because of her devotion to her father, her husband must be able to accommodate to Mr. Woodhouse. Thus, Mr. Knightley is the perfect match.

Just as a series of simple declarative sentences becomes monotonous, so many long, involved sentences, one after another, can be tiring. Variety of sentence structure breaks the monotony and lets the writer use the short declarative sentence for emphasis, as in the last example.

Repetition is another device ordinarily useful for transitions and emphasis but subject to abuse. Used carelessly, repetition impresses the reader as the product of a dull plodding mind:

The reader of *Emma* wants Emma to marry someone so she will not be trapped into the dull role of a single woman in her society. The reader wants Emma to marry a man who is worthy of her, and the reader wants that man to be considerate of her father. Mr. Knightley is eligible because he is worthy, because he has been considerate of her father, and because he has already demonstrated his concern for her.

We can recognize the problem in this paragraph as soon as we realize how much it could be shortened without diminishing the content or creating confusion.

Needless repetition is not the only reason for pruning. Crutch words and phrases which come easily to many writers under the pressure of composition can also be pruned to strengthen the prose. Frequently used crutch words and phrases include:

There is

> The house on the corner needs painting.
> rather than
> There is a house on the corner that needs painting.

Due to the fact that

> The siding will be damaged by moisture penetrating where the paint has peeled.
> rather than
> The siding will be damaged due to the fact that moisture can penetrate where the paint is peeling.

Who is

> The frank man can be trusted.
> rather than
> The man who is frank can be trusted.
> John, the boy across the street, climbs fences.
> rather than
> John, who is the boy across the street, climbs fences.

The fact that

> My trip to Brazil . . . .
> rather than
> The fact that I had gone to Brazil . . . .

Which is

> This mystery story is set in Galena.
> rather than
> This novel is a mystery story which is set in Galena

Another form of wordiness in research papers comes from unnecessary or careless qualifying. Because the researcher must be scrupulous to separate facts from opinions and to refrain from overstating his case, he may be tempted to qualify unnecessarily his argument or interpretation. The grotesque example of this is the paper beginning "In my opinion, I think . . . ." A writer's interpretation of his data will pervade his report , both in his presentation and selection of facts. He is obligated to represent the facts accurately. But a careful, honest representation of facts does not require unnecessary and debilitating qualification of interpretation. Thus, "It appears" and "It seems" are quite as tentative as "It appears to me" or "It seems to me" and the shorter forms avoid the intrusion of an insecure author. If the facts support a forthright, positive statement, then the statement should be left forthright and positive, without a "perhaps" which leaves the author on the fence.

The need to eliminate wordiness is not a need to eliminate specific, concrete language. An abstract statement is seldom more concise than a similar statement in concrete terms. Look again at the paragraph from Muriel Beadle's *A Child's Mind:*

> As the varying cultural patterns of the world's peoples attest, young humans are enormously adaptable, and older humans are exceptionally faithful to the ways of their forebears. A baby can learn to sleep upright and tightly swaddled, or prone and without a cover. If his mother elects not to carry him in a sling on her back during the day and keep him in her bed at night, he adjusts very well to spending long solitary periods in his crib or playpen. As a newborn, he feeds whenever he is hungry or according to some externally imposed schedule, and grows into a pattern of eating once a day or five times a day — not because such behavior is best in any absolute sense but because it is customary in his culture.

Notice how stilted the paragraph becomes when the concepts are stated in general abstract terms:

People perpetuate the patterns their forebears have passed onto them. Sleeping patterns in babies persist through generations and are culturally determined. Feeding patterns of the young tend to be uniform throughout a society because of the power of cultural patterns which are not absolute values in themselves.

The specific language of the original paragraph is more convincing and interesting than the generalizations of the second paragraph, which resembles more an outline than a fully developed idea.

Nouns which refer directly to concrete objects and active verbs can have emotional power as well as convincing specificity. Thus, when Lear, who has been beggared by the daughters he made queens, meets the ragged Edgar, his compassionate response is:

"Didst thou give all to thy daughters, and art thou come to this?"

Not:
Is your pitiable state the result of filial ingratitude?

The same principle can be found in *The Letters of Ezra Pound 1907-1941*, edited by D.D. Paige (New York: Harcourt Brace and Company, 1950). Affirming that the virtues of good poetry are those of good prose, Pound wrote Harriet Monroe: "Language is made out of concrete things. General expressions in non-concrete terms are a laziness; . . . ." (p. 49)

Earlier in the same letter Pound says that the precision characteristic of good writing is the ". . . result of concentrated attention to what is writing. The test of the writer is his ability for such concentration AND for his power to stay concentrated till he gets to the end . . . ." Unfortunately, the writer of a term paper or thesis is not to the end when he has seen his internal dialogue, Pound's "what is writing," complete and refined, for the writer must still prepare the manuscript in an accepted conventional form. To that form we turn now.

TWO — FORM

The Final Draft

Once you have finished all of your revising and editing, you are ready to prepare a final copy of the paper or to submit a legible draft of the thesis or dissertation to your advisor. Many students turn in portions of the thesis as they are completed for their advisors to read and comment on. If you have not done this, you will have to prepare a legible draft for approval, because it is foolhardy to prepare the final copy before you and your advisor have agreed on the revisions to be made.

The draft from which you or someone else prepares the final typescript should be as legible as possible, for the more difficult the text is to read and the more often you or your typist must go to a separate page for an insertion, the more mistakes are likely to appear in the final copy. Also, if you are typing the final copy yourself, and if it is psychologically possible, you should refrain from revising or tinkering as you type. Perhaps the greatest advantage to having someone else type the final copy is that he cannot tinker and can, therefore, devote full attention to the typing itself.

The forms prescribed for term papers, theses, and dissertations are designed to make them easy to read. In general, the forms for academic papers follow the form desired by book publishers and editors of scholarly journals, particularly in such things as style, spacing, margins, and paper. The most significant conflict between academic and professional models is the rule for single spacing footnotes and long quotations — publishers want everything double spaced. As for the minutiae of notes and bibliography, there are many forms for different publishers, for different disciplines, and for different schools. For economic reasons, however, many publishers are discouraging the use of notes and bibliography altogether. Just as the notes and bibliography are the most difficult part of the manuscript to type, so they are the most expensive for the publisher to produce.

Although there is disparity on the minutiae of form, particularly in the case of documentation, many of the rules for form are universal, and once you have mastered the basic form for footnote and bibliography, it is easy enough to make small adjustments for one or another style. Here we will try to provide the standards of form usually set for academic papers and a single consistent pattern for footnotes and bibliography. For the notes and bibliography we will provide the fullest form in general use and then indicate ways in which that form is sometimes abbreviated as well as a means for keeping the number of notes to a minimum without compromising the integrity of the scholarship.

All of the rules here assume that the final copy is typewritten. Of course, there is no question of this in the case of theses and dissertations. There should be no question of it for the extended term paper or seminar report for which this manual is also designed. It is an imposition to ask someone to read a long handwritten manuscript, and if a student has decided that he does not need to know how to type, college is as good a place as any for him to accept the financial responsibility and inconvenience of having someone else do his typing for him.

Academic papers are typed on 8½x11 inch paper with margins of at least 1½ inches at the left and 1 inch at the top, bottom, and right. The extra space at the left allows for binding in the cases of theses and dissertations and for comments by the instructor in the case of less august documents. Completing the manuscript can be done in four stages: (1) the text; (2) the notes; (3) the bibliography; (4) the preliminary matter. In practice the notes should be prepared before the final text is typed, for if the notes are typed at the bottom of the page, they will be typed at the same time the text is typed, and if they are typed at the end of the paper or of individual chapters, preparing them in advance will show which can be eliminated by including bibliographical information in the text. Each stage is discussed in the order in which it appears in the final manuscript, even though the preliminary material is usually prepared last.

THE PRELIMINARY MATTER

The preliminary material includes in this order: the title page; the preface; the table of contents; any list of tables, charts, illustrations, or maps that may be necessary.

The title page should be appropriate to the scope of the paper and the institution. It seems pedantic and stuffy to garnish the title page of a ten-page term paper with the words, "A term paper submitted in partial fulfillment of the course requirements of Phenomenology, Philosophy 351." A similar statement is, however, regularly included in the title page of theses and dissertations, and might be appropriate for an honors project or a report on independent study. Many universities have very specific requirements for the format and spacing of the title page of theses and dissertations. Examples of accepted theses and dissertations can be examined in the library of the institution for which a student desires a model. An example of one form is in the appendix. For a term paper, the title of the paper typed in capitals and centered near the top of the page, the author's name in suitably humble capitals and lower case letters centered in the middle of the page, plus the course title, the instructor's name, and the date, all centered at the bottom, should suffice. An example of such a title page is also included in the appendix.

The preface, if there is one, includes whatever the author wants to say about the work which is not included in the text itself, along with any expressions of gratitude he wants to make. Ordinarily, a preface would not be necessary in the case of a term paper, and, if a student had nothing to say about the background and preparation of either the research or the report that was not included in the text, and if he had received no special or extraordinary help from instructors, librarians, or institutions, a preface might be unnecessary in a dissertation. When there is a preface it follows the title page, and its first page has the capitalized, centered heading "PREFACE." Since the preliminary material is numbered in small roman numerals, with the title page unnumbered but taking the place of i, the preface begins on page ii and is so numbered at the bottom center of the page.

The table of contents is also titled at the center top of the page in capitals. It cannot, of course, be prepared until the final manuscript is typed with all the pages numbered. A student usually has considerable leeway in how extensive he makes the table of contents. He may choose simply to give the chapter titles and their beginning page numbers, plus the page numbers of any appendixes and the bibliography. Many people, however, choose to indicate more extensively what is included in the chapters, either through a summary of the contents, indented below the chapter title, or through the use of subtopics, with pages indicated if the subtopics are clearly marked in the text. Examples of each of these are found in the appendix. Some instructors desire an outline. If you are substituting an outline for a table of contents, remember:

1. The whole outline should be consistently either a topic outline or a sentence outline.

2. Headings are subdivided and enumerated first with large roman numerals, then with capital letters, then with arabic numbers, then with lower case letters, and last with small roman numerals.

3. One heading at any level is bad form. This rule is based on the argument that on each level the headings represent subdivisions of the larger topic under which they are listed, and anything that is divided must be divided into at least two parts.

If you have numerous tables, charts, illustrations, or maps, you may want to number them and include a list of their locations after the table of contents. Each such list should be separately typed, separately numbered, and appropriately headed — again in the center of the top of the page in capital letters.

THE TEXT

After the preliminaries, the pages are numbered continuously with arabic numbers. Pages that have a major heading at the top of the page, such as the beginning of chapters and the titled appendixes, are numbered at the center of the bottom page, two spaces below the bottom margin. Other pages in the text are numbered in the upper right hand corner, two spaces above the top line, with the number within the right hand margin. The heading for the chapter number is centered in the first line below the margin and typed in capitals. Double space is left between it and the heading giving the chapter title, and double or triple space is left between the title and the first line of text:

CHAPTER II

THE NEW DEAL

Here would begin the first line of the chapter.

The text is double spaced except for footnotes, long quotations, and tables. In the text, footnotes are indicated by arabic numerals raised one half space above the line, immediately following the last word to be noted. The number comes at the end of a summary or paraphrase and directly follows the closing quotation mark in the case of a direct quotation. Thus, it may well come in the middle of a sentence rather than at the end, but if the last word is followed by a punctuation mark, the footnote numeral follows all punctuation marks except dashes. Here are some examples of the placement of footnote numerals with a description of what the reader would expect to find in the note:

The League of Women Voters of Illinois affirm the need for positive action on the state level to encourage every community to provide its share of low and moderate income housing.[1]

[1] The note should indicate where the reader can find an official League statement of its position on low and moderate income housing.

The League of Women Voters of Illinois believe that "carefully screened volunteers could be used for probation and parole."[2]

[2] The note should provide the exact source of the quoted words in an official League statement.

"The ability of the Viet Cong continuously to rebuild their units and to make good their losses . . ."[3] was a mystery to U.S. military officials.

[3] The note should identify the exact source of the words of the military official who is being used as an example of U.S. military attitudes. The context should be consistent with the author's use of the quotation — the official should be baffled by the Viet Cong capabilities.

In term papers footnotes are numbered consecutively from beginning to end. In works with chapters, footnotes are numbered consecutively for each chapter, each chapter beginning with footnote one.

If footnotes are typed at the bottom of the page, the notes should be typed above the bottom margin, so space must be left for them. Usually, two spaces (triple space) are left between the last line of text and the first note, with the break emphasized by a typed line twenty spaces long:

Here would be the last line of text.

[4] John Doe, The Development of American Trade (New York: Finley Press, 1957), p. 87.

[5] Brown, Trade Barriers, p. 73.

As you can see from the example, a space is left between footnotes.

Special rules of typographical form apply to quotations as well as to footnote numerals and placement. Any quotation three typed lines or shorter can be typed run-on in the text. Then the quotation is set off by quotation marks:

Shakespeare's Brutus said, "The good is oft interred with their bones,"

but in the case of this statesman . . . .

(Notice that a reference note is unnecessary for a famous quotation when its use is incidental to the purpose of the paper. The exact location of the quotation would be necessary, however, in a discussion of the play.) In the case of poetry, line breaks are indicated by a virgule.(/):

The depth of Frost's pessimism is revealed in the final couplet of his

sonnet "Design," "What but design of darkness to appall? — / If   / If

design govern in a thing so small."[6]

If more than three lines of poetry are quotes, however, even if they could be compacted into fewer than three lines of text by use of virgules, the quotation will look neater if single spaced and indented. Any quotation longer than three typed lines should be introduced by a colon, indented to paragraph indention, and single spaced beginning two lines below the last line of text. Since the indented block of single spaced typing sets off the quotation, quotation marks are not used.

If you want to quote less than a complete sentence or paragraph in your paper, you may do so, but since all quotations must be accurate, omissions, should be indicated clearly in the text. At the beginning of a sentence or within a sentence an omission is indicated by an ellipsis mark, that is three spaced periods (. . .). If the omission is at the end of a sentence ending with a period, four spaced periods (. . . .) indicate the ellipsis mark plus the final period. Therefore, if the sentence ends with a question mark or exclamation point, that punctuation follows the ellipsis, which is still marked by three spaced periods (. . . ?) . If a paragraph is omitted in a long quotation which is single spaced and indented, the omission is indicated by a line of spaced dots:

Those religious poems which are structured either as statements or as

arguments I call discursive, those which recreate a specific religious

experience I call representational.

. . . .

The discursive poems in the Harley manuscript include five poems about

repentance and death, two poems which endeavor to persuade the

audience to love Christ, and four vernacular verse prayers.

The same line of spaced periods is used to indicate the omission of a line or more of verse. In short quotations included in the text, such long omissions are indicated by separate sets of quotation marks:

The critic classifies religious poems as discursive and representational. The former ". . . are structured either as statements or arguments." "The discursive poems in the Harley manuscript include five poems about repentance and death . . . ."8

Insertions or corrections are indicated by square brackets, and since few typewriters have keys for these, they must be added by hand in black ink. For example:

"He [John Doe] argues for a stimulus-response pattern for language learning."

"Scientists' and philosophers' descriptions of the scientific method differ astonishingly. The scientist is usually arguing from *experience*, the philosopher from *logic."* [emphasis mine]

Also, should you want to disclaim a minor error in the quotation, the disclaimer or correct information is indicated in square brackets:

"Ben Johnson's [sic] plays remain a staple of repertory groups," or

"Ben Johnson's plays remain a staple of repertory groups." [the original mispells Jonson] or

"Ben Johnson's [thus in the original] plays remain a staple of repertory groups.

If you are quoting material printed before English spelling was standardized, you will want to decide if you are going to represent the original exactly and follow the old spelling, or if you are going to standardize according to modern principles. Should you choose to do the latter, you should indicate so in the text, in an explanatory note, or in the preface.

Accuracy demands that the punctuation of a quotation be reproduced exactly. However, punctuation marks within ellipses are omitted, and modern American practice is to include all commas and periods within the quotation marks, whether in the quotation or simply required by the context. Indeed, some scholars omit ellipses at the beginning and ends of quotations that make grammatical sentences without the quoted parts when such omissions do not significantly change the sense of the passage.

While this manual does not attempt to include a complete description of the appropriate style of punctuation for academic papers, we can review a few more problems which are common to, but not confined to, research reports and which even advanced students may find useful.

The first such problem is a rule with many exceptions. In the text, single numbers of less than three digits are spelled out (sixty) and numbers of three or more digits are typed with numerals or figures (1,250). Now for the exceptions: dates, addresses, and time of day followed by a.m. or p.m. are not spelled out. Nor are numbers used for decimals, measurements (4 by 6 inch cards), dollars and cents ($4.25), and percentages (7% or seven per cent). In addition, in paragraphs where many numbers appear, especially for statistical purposes, all the numbers are typed as numerals:

> As of June 1, 1976, 325 families in Blooming Grove were on welfare. Of these families, only 33 had been on welfare for more than 2 years, and permanent physical disability of a family member was a factor in 30 of those families. A survey of the families which had received welfare for less than 2 years indicated that 75 of them could provide for themselves if adequate, economical daycare were available to them.

But in less statistical writing, numbers are spelled out according to the rules:

> In two years the three brothers accumulated seventy-five impressionist paintings. Thirty of these were stored in a rural summer home which was destroyed by fire at 7:00 a.m. on January 5, 1976.

A second stylistic problem arises with the use of foreign words. The rule says that foreign words are underlined. However, many words have been assimilated into the English language. Some, like "fabliau" and "minutia," have been assimilated recently enough to maintain the plurals of the original language ("fabliaux" and "minutiae"), but they are included in *Webster's Seventh Collegiate Dictionary* and may, therefore, be used without underlining. Any good English dictionary can provide a standard for usage, but since not all such dictionaries agree, to be fully consistent, you should use only one.

For ease of reading as much as for stylistic purposes, abbreviations should be avoided. If, however, you are going to refer to something that is often abbreviated and has a long title, then spell out the title the first time it appears and give the abbreviation you will use: ". . . the United Nations Children's Fund (hereafter UNICEF)."

Underlining is used to indicate the title of anything that is ordinarily published separately, including books, pamphlets, periodicals, newspapers, plays, motion pictures, anthologies, and any poetic work long enough to be published separately, such as <u>Paradise Lost.</u> Quotation marks are used around titles of works that are usually published in something else, such as magazine or journal articles, short poems, short lectures, newspaper articles, short stories, chapter titles, and the titles of radio or television programs. The titles of unpublished works such as dissertations, theses, minutes, or multilithed or dittoed reports are also marked by quotation marks. The names of the books of the Bible are not marked with either quotation marks or underlining. A normally underlined title within an underlined title is marked by quotation marks, as in <u>Interpretations of "Piers Plowman."</u>

Finally, a note on breakover words at the ends of lines. Words of more than one syllable may be divided between syllables at the end of a line if all three conditions apply:

1. at least three letters carry over to the next line
2. more than one letter is left on the first line
3. a hyphenated word is not divided at a point other than the hyphen.

Since the word must be divided between syllables, you may find you have to check a dictionary for the appropriate point to breakover. However, the time taken to look up the word is seldom worth the space saved or the improved appearance of a more perfectly aligned margin at the right, and two or three empty spaces at the end of a line are far less distracting than an awkwardly divided word. So, when in doubt, don't divide the word.

REFERENCE NOTES

In preparation of the final typescript, the reference material, that is the footnotes and bibliography, presents the most problems. A concern for the form of notes and bibliography can become a time-consuming preoccupation. Suppress pedantry by remembering that the purpose of the reference notes and bibliography is to give the reader all the information he needs to check the facts and sources used in the preparation of the paper. Completeness and consistency are essential, and making the information as accessible and undistracting as possible is a courtesy to the reader.

Reference notes are placed at the bottom of the page, at the ends of chapters, or, in the case of short papers, at the end of the paper. Most instructors will accept endnotes in place of footnotes, and it is certainly easier for the student to type the notes at the end of the chapter or paper than at the foot of the page. When the student takes this convenient road, however, he should remember that every footnote numeral on the page may mean an interruption in the reading of the text while the reader goes back to the end to check the note. Except for theses and dissertations, which are ultimately bound, the student can make up for the inconvenience of endnotes by turning the paper in held together by a paperclip. If he does this the instructor can place the notes next to the text while reading the paper. Endnotes are particularly inconvenient for theses and dissertations, which are bound and reproduced on microfilm. Indeed, some universities insist on notes at the bottom of the page. The student whose university does permit endnotes, and who chooses to use them, should at least make every effort to minimize the number of notes and to incorporate reference information in the text.

Endnotes and footnotes have the same typographical form. The first line of the note begins at paragraph indentation with the number of the note raised one half space above the line. Each individual note is single spaced, but double space is left between the last line of one note and the first line of the next.

Any discussion of the form of footnotes and bibliography is detailed and technical. Here we will begin with the form for the simplest sort of book — a first edition, unedited, in the original language, published commercially in a single volume without being part of a series. We will then show how any or all of these complications are added to the basic form. After the discussion of books, we will describe the form used for citing articles in journals, magazines, and newspapers, the form used for public documents; and, finally, the form used for unpublished works. Having shown the complete form for footnotes, we will then comment on how that form is routinely abbreviated in some fields, and how the number and length of footnotes can be reduced in any paper by including bibliographical information in the text. The discussion of notes will end with the standard methods of citing sources after the first full reference note. Our discussion of the form for entries in bibliographies will simply describe the differences between bibliography entries and reference notes. The sample bibliography in the appendix will be a bibliography of all the examples used in the discussion of footnotes.

Although this guide attempts to be comprehensive enough to provide the information needed for a large number of students using a wide range of resources, there will be many examples of bibliographic problems which are not explicitly covered, and there will be cases where individual judgments must be made. Then common sense must dictate the accommodation of form to be made or the emphasis chosen. For example, books sometimes list on their title page both corporate sponsors and individual authors, as in the case of *The Limits of Growth,* subtitled *A Report for the Club of Rome's*

Project on the Predicament of Mankind (New York: Universe Books, 1972), which lists a group of authors beginning with Donella H. Meadows. The Library of Congress provides two author cards for this book — "Club of Rome," and "Donella H. Meadows [and others]." For a reference note, however, you must select only one for the first position, which will get the primary emphasis, and which will serve as the identifying phrase for all subsequent notes. Since publicity and reviews have given more prominence to the Club of Rome than to the actual authors, it is likely that your reader will more easily recognize the "Club of Rome" designation, and it should probably be selected for the author spot.

This is only one example of the choices the research writer must make in preparing the documentation for his report. The most complete guide cannot make these choices for you, and one that is too complete and too rigid may dictate a form that is ludicrously inappropriate in your particular situation. The forms here are offered as a guide, but you must be prepared to accommodate the forms to the idiosyncrasies of your sources and research and to the needs of your audience.

FIRST REFERENCE TO A BOOK

The basic form for the footnote for a book with an uncomplicated origin or publication history is:

footnote number
The author's complete name. Title of the Book or Pamphlet (Publication Information), exact location of the citation.

An example is:
[9]Margaret Mead, Blackberry Winter: My Earlier Years (New York: William Morrow & Company, Inc., 1972), p. 142.

The author's name should be as complete as possible. If the title page does not give the full name of the author, then the catalog card in the library often does. Information which is added to that found on the title page is enclosed in square brackets. Thus, if you discover that J.T. Jones on the title page was Jeremiah Thaddeus Jones, the author entry in the note would be J[eremiah] T[haddeus] Jones. The full name makes a book easier to find for the reader who wants to check a reference or to learn more from a source you have cited. Trying to find "J. R. R. Smith" in a large card catalog can be frustrating and time consuming. But, since the full name of the author is primarily for identification, the initialed form on the title page can be retained for prominent individuals about whom there would be no question, such as T.S. Eliot, J.R.R. Tolkien, and B.F. Skinner. Thus, too, it is ordinarily unnecessary to search for the full names when the name would not be the first choice for tracing the material, as in the case of journal articles.

If a book has two authors, both authors are listed as they appear on the title page:

[10]Albert H. Marckwardt and James L. Rosier, Old English Literature (New York: W.W. Norton & Company, 1972), p. 75.

If more than three authors are listed on the title page, then only the first is given in the note, plus an indication that there are others — either "et al.," an abbreviation for *et alii* meaning " and others," or the English "and others":

[11]Charles R. Frank, Jr., and others, Assisting Developing Countries: Problem of Debts, Burden-sharing, Jobs and Trade, Overseas Development Council Studies 1 (New York: Praeger Publishers, 1972), p. 179.

A committee, corporation, or government office may be responsible for a book for which no author is given on the title page. Since the corporate entity is responsible for the book, the name of the entity is used for the author:

[12]Drug Abuse Survey Project, Dealing with Drug Abuse: A Report to the Ford Foundation (New York: Praeger, 1972), p. 302.

As described earlier, a book may have both a corporate author and an individually named author, in which case you must decide which is more important and list accordingly:

[13]Club of Rome, The Limits of Growth: A Report for the Club of Rome's Project on the Predicament of Mankind, by Donella H. Meadows and others (New York: Universe Books, 1972), p. 35.

Or

[14]Donella H. Meadows and others, The Limits of Growth: A Report for the Club of Rome's Project on the Predicament of Mankind (New York: Universe Books, 1972), p. 35.

If the author of the work you are citing is unknown, then there is no author entry and the note begins with the title:

[15]Sir Gawain and the Green Knight, trans. Theodore Howard Banks, Jr. (New York: Appleton-Century-Crofts, Inc., 1929), 11. 2052-59.

If the name listed on the title page is a pseudonym and you wish to identify the author, the real name can be supplied in square brackets:

[16]Michael Innes [J.I.M. Stewart], <u>One-Man Show</u> (New York: Dodd, Mead & Company, 1952), p. 51.

The second major element of the note is the title of the book or pamphlet. Usually all of the title and subtitle is given, but when the title is exceptionally long, perhaps longer than two typed lines, an innocuous segment can be omitted as long as the omission is marked by ellipsis points. Within certain limits, the note reproduces the punctuation of the title on the title page. One such limit concerns capitalization. In some books the title is printed entirely in capital letters, but the title in the notes is typed in a combination of capitals and lower case letters. The most common pattern is that used in the examples in this manual, that is, the first and last words and all words except conjunctions, prepositions, and articles are capitalized. It is also acceptable to follow the pattern used on library catalog cards. In that pattern the first word is capitalized, and beyond the first word, only those words which would be capitalized in the text, such as proper names, are capitalized. Another modification of the punctuation of the title occurs when there is no punctuation between the main title and the subtitle. Fill such a hiatus with a colon unless some other mark is clearly more appropriate. Titles in foreign languages are capitalized and punctuated according to the conventions of the language.

The basic publication information, the third major element of the note, is given in parentheses in the note and includes the place of publication, the publisher, and the date of the work. In some fields the publisher is not included, and the place of publication and the date are separated by a comma, instead of a colon, in the parentheses. Like the author and title, the publication data is taken from the title page. If the information is missing and you can supply it, it is enclosed in square brackets. If the information is unavailable, this is indicated by abbreviations — "n.p." for "no place" and "n.d." for "no date." When several cities are listed on the title page, only the first is given in the note. Unless you are willing to check in *Books in Print* or the *Reference Catalogue of Current Literature* for the correct abbreviations for all the publishers you cite, give the full name of the publisher as it appears on the title page. Sometimes professional associations, institutions, and businesses publish books, and their names then appear as the publisher.

The date of the work is ordinarily the last date of copyright, which is usually given on the overleaf of the title page. If the date on the title page itself is different from the date of copyright, then either the book was copyrighted the year before it was actually issued (and the date on the title page is the date for the notes and bibliography), or, more commonly, the book is a reprint. A reprint may or may not use the same plates as the original edition, which means that page references to a reprint may or may not correspond with the original edition. If the reprint is by the original publisher, the last copyright date is given. But if a different publisher is responsible for the reprint, then the copyright date is indicated in the parentheses before the place of publication: (1955; rpt. New York: Many Books Inc., 1966). Some reprint publishers do not give the original date of publication for books which are out of copyright, and in such cases it is a good idea to check the Library of Congress *National Union Catalog* or similar source to determine the original publication date, because information in a book published fifty years ago needs to be evaluated differently from information in a book published only a year or two ago; the older book may have been superseded. Also, giving the first date of publication plus the date for the edition you are using tells the reader that the same quotation or information can be found in either 1955 edition or the 1966 reprint.

In a single volume work, the location of the citation is simply the page or pages where the information or quotation can be found. If all the information is on one page, then the abbreviation "p." precedes the appropriate number. If two or more consecutive pages are given, the abbreviation "pp." for "pages" is used. A list of the exact pertinent pages is far more useful to the reader than these abbreviations, which are sometimes used:

"pp. 65 et seq." for "page 65 and following."
"pp. 65 f." for "page 65 and the following page."
"pp. 65 ff." for "page 65 and the following pages."
"pp. 65 et passim" for "page 65 and here and there throughout the work."

Note that the second form is no improvement over "pp. 65-66," and the other three examples are less informative than an exact reference such as "pp. 65-69" or "pp. 65-67, 69, 73-75, and 80."

In poetry the line numbers are given when the lines are numbered in the text cited. The abbreviations "l" for "line" and "ll" for "lines" precede the number(s). When a long poem has been subdivided into books or cantos, the book or canto number, in large roman numerals, precedes the line number. Only the numbers, separated by a period, are used — III. 25-26. If the larger units are subdivided into smaller units within which the lines are numbered, the pattern is to use large roman numerals for the largest unit, small roman numerals for the next largest, and arabic numerals for the line numbers — "IV. ii. 25-30." Quotations to plays follow the same format to indicate the act. scene, and lines — "III. iv. 25" for "Act III, scene iv, line 25."

Multivolume works, works with editors and translators, works which have been revised or have appeared in more than one edition, and works published in series all require citations which include this information, all of which helps a curious reader readily identify the work and find the passage to which you are referring.

Leaving aside for a moment the question of the multivolume work, the other three situations can be handled in this pattern:

footnote number
   Author's name, *Title*, editor or translator, edition number, series title and number (Publication data), exact location of citation.

Consider the following examples:

[17]Ernst Robert Curtius, European Literature and the Latin Middle Ages, trans. Willard R. Trask, The Bollingen Library (1953; rpt. New York: Harper & Row, Publishers, 1963), pp. 39-42.

Note that 1953 is the date that Pantheon Books published the first edition of the translation for the Bollingen Foundation. If the writer citing the book believed the date of publication of the German edition would be of interest to his readers, he could add to the note, "Originally published as *Europaische Literatur und lateinisches Mittelalter (*Bern, 1948)."

[18]"Beowulf"; Reproduced in Facsimile from the Unique Manuscript, British Museum MS. Cotton Vitellius A.xv, transliteration and notes by Julius Zupitza, 2nd ed., Early English Text Society No. 245 (London: Oxford University Press, 1959), p. 21.

The abbreviations "ed." and "trans." mean "edited by" and "translated by," and since, in this example, Zupitza transliterated rather than translated, his special function is spelled out unambiguously. Also note that the number of a volume in a series is given when the series is numbered.

If you are citing the work of the editor or translator rather than the author, then the editor's name appears in the author's place in the note, and, if the author's name does not appear in the title, it is given in the place of the editor with "by" indicating the author's role.

[19]Peter Allt and Russell K. Alspach, eds., The Variorum Edition of the Poems of W.B. Yeats (New York: The Macmillan Company, 1957) p. 354.

The edition number is usually indicated clearly on the title page. If not, the information is given in the copyright statement on the reverse side.

Normally you are expected to use the last revised edition of a work for your research, unless special reasons of scholarship dictate using an earlier edition. Such reasons should be clear from the text or made clear in the note. Classic works of literature, philosophy, and history are exceptions to this rule. If such a work is out of copyright any publisher can produce an edition. Often there are many cheap editions of such works, editions designed to be sold at newsstands. Rarely are these editions satisfactory for academic work, and the researcher is expected to use a standard scholarly edition. Not only are the texts of such editions likely to be more accurate, but libraries which will not attempt to acquire every popular edition of a book such as *Huckleberry Finn* will be certain to have the standard scholarly edition of the work. Thus, your reader will be able to check you more readily in the library if you have used the standard edition.

Naturally, if the book is the text for a seminar or advanced course for which the paper is being prepared, you will cite the edition assigned for the course, unless your point involves a difference among editions. Finally, in the case of books produced before the introduction of stereotype in the early nineteenth century, if no modern standard edition exists, you may need to learn about early book making practices and technical bibliography.

How you handle a multivolume work of prose in a note depends upon your emphasis. You may omit indicating the number of volumes, and merely indicate the inclusive dates of publication, and then indicate the number of the volume which you are citing:

[20]John Smith, The History and Tradition of Centralia County (Springfield, Illinois: Marigold Press, 1857 – 1865), III, 35-37.

This is the least precise way to cite the sources, for it does not tell the reader how many volumes are in the work or when,. exactly, volume three was published.

A second method for the same reference, places the number of volumes before the publication information:

[21]John Smith, The History and Tradition of Centralia County, 4 vols. (Springfield, Illinois: Marigold Press, 1857-1865), III, 35-37

Should you think that your reader would find the exact date of the volume more useful than the total number of volumes, you can put the volume number before the publication information, and then give only the date of publication for that particular volume:

[22]John Smith, The History and Tradition of Centralia County, vol. III (Springfield, Illinois: Marigold Press, 1862), pp. 35-37.

Notice that when the volume number and page number are together, no abbreviations of "volume" or "page" are necessary. Which of the three forms you choose should depend on the needs of your audience.

If the volume is separately titled, or if a multivolume work contains volumes by different authors, the title of the collection is given:

[23]W[illiam] L[indsay] Renwick. English Literature 1789-1815 in The Oxford History of English Literature, ed. F[rank] P[ercy] Wilson and Bonamy Dobree, vol. IX (Oxford: The Clarendon Press, 1963), pp. 78-79.

Similarly, if you are citing an article, poem, or story in a collection of some sort, the author and title of the separate part are given first in the note:

[24]N.K. Coghill, "Love and 'Foul Delight': Some Contrasted Attitudes" in Patterns of Love and Courtesy: essays in Memory of C.S. Lewis, ed. John Lawlor (London: Edward Arnold (Publishers) Ltd., 1966), p. 151.

If the collection you are using is an anthology of previously published journal articles, citing the bibliographical data for the original publication gives the reader the date of the article as well as a second source for it:

[25]J.R.R. Tolkien, "The Monsters and The Critics," Proceedings of the British Academy, 22 (2936), 245-295, rpt. in An Anthology of Beowulf Criticism, ed. Lewis E. Nicholson (Notre Dam, Indiana: University of Notre Dam Press, 1963), p. 91.

Standard reference books arranged alphabetically are handled somewhat differently. In the case of a signed article in an encyclopedia, the author's name, usually discovered by tracing the initials at the end of the article to the list of contributors, is given first, followed by the title of the article, the name of the reference work, and the year of publication. Since the same article may appear in an edition published in a different year, and since volume numbering and pagination may not be consistent in printings or editions containing the same article or item, the title or topic is the most convenient reference for the reader·

[26]M.M. Hueller et al, "Hymns and Hymnals," The New Catholic Encyclopedia, 1967.

[27]Oxford English Dictionary, 1933, s.v. scatterbrain.

[28]Lionel Cust, "Gentileschi, Orazio," Dictionary of National Biography, 1908.

If you are doing a close analysis of an ancient or modern classic, then your first reference note for the work will give the complete bibliographical information of the edition you are using. For the location of passages you may have to cite page numbers, but you should prefer a method which would allow your reader to locate the passage in another edition. Thus, when citing a Shakespeare play, cite the act, scene, and line, rather than the page of a particular edition. Similarly, when citing the long eighteenth-century novel *Tom Jones*, you could cite book and chapter as well as the page in the standard edition. If, however, you are citing a classic work for a purpose such that your reader need not know the exact edition, then you may simply cite the work and the place, not the page, in the work, without giving a specific edition:

> [29]Shakespeare, Hamlet, II.iii.35-37.
>
> [30]Virgil, Aeneid. VI.417-421.
>
> [31]Aristotle, Metaphysics, XIII.4.

Similarly, one need not encumber the reader with page numbers or editions for the Bible. Indeed, all that is needed is the title of the book, not underlined, the chapter and verse. In some cases you might want to indicate the version.

> [32]Psalms 22:1 or [32]Ps 22:1
>
> [33]I Timothy 6:2 or [33]I Tim 6:2
>
> [34]Isaiah 12:5 or [34]Is 12:5 (Revised Standard Version)

It is better to place short citations like these parenthetically in the text than to interrupt the reader's attention with a note, but the form for the parenthetical citation is the same as for the note.

FIRST REFERENCE TO A PERIODICAL

Fortunately, citations to periodicals have fewer variations and complications than those for books. The basic pattern is:

> footnote number
>
> Author's name, "Full title of the article,"
> Name of the periodical, Volume number, issue number (Date),
> Page number (s) of the citation.

Good sense determines how much to include for volume number, issue number, and date. You should include the information necessary to locate the passage easily. For the many journals that page the issues of a volume continuously, the issue number is unnecessary. Indeed, for journals which page the volume continuously and whose volume year coincides with the calendar year, it would be logical to give only the volume number, but it is customary to give the year and the volume as a precaution against error. On the other hand, popular magazines and newspapers begin each issue with page one, so for them the exact date is crucial. Consider the following examples:

[35]Matthew W. Finkin, "Collective Bargaining and University Government," AAUP Bulletin, 57 (1971), 151.

[36]Roger Sale, "England's Parnassus: C.S. Lewis, Charles Williams, and J.R.R. Tolkein," The Hudson Review, 17 (Summer, 1964), 204.

The Hudson Review's volume year does not coincide with the calendar year, hence the year alone is not sufficient.

[37]Annie Dillard, "The Force that Drives the Flower," The Atlantic, 232 (November, 1973), 74.

[38]Horace Freeland Judson, "A Reporter at Large (Heroin in Great Britain — 1)," The New Yorker, September 24, 1973, p. 78.

One could give the volume number in this reference, but that is not usually done when an exact date is given. Note that when there is no volume number given, the abbreviations "p." or "pp." precede the page number.

[39]Marilyn Bender, "The Very Private Pritzkers: Chicago Deal Makers in Publishing Spotlight," The New York Times, Oct. 14, 1973, sec. 3, p. 1.

Since the sections of this newspaper are paged separately the section number must be given. When the place of publication of a newspaper is not included in the title, it is given in parenthesis after the title. In some cases, the town named in the title may not be sufficient identification (almost every state in the union has a town named Springfield, for example), so the name of the state is added parenthetically.

When the author's name is not given, begin with the title of the article. In some cases, such as reviews, it is usual to include an explanatory statement:

[40]"Global Annual," anonymous review of The Statesman's Year Book 1973-74: Statistical and Historical Annual of the States of the World, ed. John Paxton, The Times Literary Supplement, Oct. 12, 1973, p. 1235.

Abbreviations are desirable in footnotes. In particular, abbreviate the titles of scholarly journals in your field with abbreviations you can expect your reader to know. For a paper on the literature in a modern language the abbreviations used in the bibliography compiled annually by the Modern Language Association would be acceptable. In medicine, the abbreviations used by *Index Medicus* could be used. By following the practice of a prestigious journal or bibliography, you ensure that the reader who does not recognize the abbreviation will know where to find what it stands for. Be more circumspect, however, where you are citing journals outside the special competence of your readers. For example, *"JAMA"* is an acceptable abbreviation for *The Journal of the American Medical Association* in a paper whose audience would be familiar with medical publications, but a student citing an article from it on Jonathan Swift's dementia for an audience of eighteenth century literary scholars would be well advised to spell out the journal title.

FIRST REFERENCE TO A GOVERNMENT DOCUMENT

The legal world has its own abbreviated form for citing government documents, statutes, and court cases. If you are writing a primarily legal paper for an audience familiar with legal citation, then you need to consult the most recent edition of *A Uniform System of Citation*, published and distributed by The Harvard Law Review Association. If, however, you are citing government documents in a less specialized context, let the following guide and common sense dictate the form of your notes:

> Footnote number
> Place of jurisdiction, Name of the branch of government or department, any subdivision thereof, Title of Document, other information needed to locate the document, place of citation.

Here are some examples:

[42]U.S., Congress, House, Committee on Un-American Acitvities, Investigation of Communist Activities in the State of California, Hearing before the Committee, 83rd Congress, 2nd sess., 1954, pt. 3, p. 54.

[43]U.S., Presidential Advisory Committee on Water Resources Policy, Water Resources Policy: a Report (Washington: Government Printing Office, 1955), p. 27.

[44]U.S., Commission on Organization of the Executive Branch

Government (1953-1955), Paperwork Management; A Report to the Congress (Washington: Government Printing Office, 1955), 1, 35.

[45]Illinois, General Assembly, Legislative Investigating Commission, The Drug Crisis: Report on Drug Abuse in Illinois to the Illinois General Assembly, 1971, p. 325.

[46]U.S. Commission on Population Growth and the American Future, Governance and Population: The Government Amplifications of Population Change, ed. A.E. Keir Nash, The Commission . . . Research Reports IV (Washington: Government Printing Office, 1972), p. 45.

Since libraries seldom list government documents under author or editor, it would be folly to list the name of the editor first in the note. Even official addresses of the chief executive may be catalogued under "U.S., President," rather than the individual name.

[47]U.S., Department of State, Amendment of Article of Agreement of the International Finance Corporation between the U.S. of America and other Governments, Treaties and International Acts Series 7683.

[48]Senator William Proxmire on the appointment of Dr. William John Fellner to the Council of Economic Advisors, Congressional Record, 119 (Oct. 18, 1973), p. S19424.

[49]Illinois General Assembly, House of Representatives High Density Housing Committee, Report, 1970.

[50]Illinois Revised Statutes, 1972 Supplement, ch. 24, paragraph 7-1-1.

[51]U.S., Constitution, article I, sec. 3.

[52]Illinois, Constitution, article II, sec. 10.

FIRST REFERENCE TO UNPUBLISHED MATERIAL

Although no manual can hope to exhaust the kinds of sources a researcher may find, we can conclude the description of citation form with examples of the notation used for the more commonly cited kinds of unpublished material, such as dissertations, letters, lectures, and unpublished papers. No matter how long the work, if it has not been published, the title is put in quotation marks, not underlined. Beyond that, provide whatever information will guide the reader to the source if it is in a library, or at least let him know where it is even if it is not publicly available. Here are the examples:

[53]Michael Gardner Crowell, "The Lexicography of Americanisms to 1880" (unpub. diss., Northwestern University, 1966), p. 36.

[54]From a MS "Autobiography" by John Russell Bartlett in the John Carter Brown Library, Brown University, Providence, Rhode Island, p. 15.

[55] From a MS letter in the Bartlett collection of the John Carter Brown Library, Brown University, Providence Rhode Island. The letter is dated at "Albany, 22d November, 1848" and signed "H. Bleecher."

[56]Paul C. Bucy, "Sitting on a Basketball," Paper presented at The Chicago Literary Club, April 16, 1973, p. 6.

[57]Letter from Edward Madigan, Representative in Congress of the 21st District of Illinois, dated September 25, 1973.

SHORTENING AND ELIMINATING NOTES

The style which we have spelled out here for footnotes to a first reference is a rather elaborate one, but one which has been generally accepted by university presses and, therefore, university graduate departments and instructors. It is used most often in its full form in the humanities, and even there it is acceptable to some schools to omit the name of the publisher. Students often object that the same information is repeated in the bibliography, and, therefore, to give a full footnote and add a bibliography is redundant. The students are right. The journals which use the full footnote rarely include a bibliography at the end of an article, and scholarly books are sometimes published without a bibliography too. In defense of redundancy we can only point out that a complete footnote is a convenience for the reader who wants to check the author or for the reader whose interest has been aroused by a particular point in the report. On the other hand, any researcher soon discovers how useful a complete bibliography is at the end of a book, and how much easier it is to use than the notes. Surely he can imagine that an instructor might want quickly to review his student's sources while evaluating the report, and for that purpose a bibliography at the end is convenient, even though complete information has been given in the notes.

The redundancy of using a full footnote form and providing a bibliography has been eliminated in many scientific fields. In the physical sciences and in some social sciences, a full list of works cited is given at the end of the paper with complete bibliographical information for each work.

References in the paper, either in the text or in footnotes, merely give the information needed to find the work in the list of references at the end and the exact place of the citation in the reference. Sometimes the date of the work is also given in the note. Unfortunately, there is no one pattern for this abbreviated method of citation. Should your field be one in which abbreviated form is acceptable, you will need to find a source which spells out which of the many variations applies to you.

Anyone, in any field, can shorten his footnotes and reduce the number of them by judiciously including bibliographical material in the text of the report. If, for example, you give the full name of the author in the text, you need not give his name in the note; you may begin with the title. If you give the full name and the complete title in the text, you need include only the publication information in the note, and if that information can be stated briefly, it can be included in the text).

The more information you include in the text the less often your reader will have to look at the notes and the fewer interruptions he will have in following your argument. Remember that a footnote numeral does not indicate whether or not substantive comments or explanations are included in the note. Since many typists charge extra for typing footnotes, the fewer footnotes the less expense for a professionally typed paper or thesis. If your work is to be published, and some graduate papers and dissertations are, the publisher will probably urge you to eliminate as many footnotes as possible. Finally, on a practical level, if you regularly include reference material in your text as you write you will have a far easier time preparing the final draft, because (1) no quotation or citation will have become separated from a note indicating its source and (2) you will have greatly cut down the chore of preparing footnotes, since you will have fewer, perhaps none, to prepare. No research paper, not even that onerous and endangered species found in Freshman English, is written for the sake of the footnotes. Neither the best researched nor the best documented paper is distinguished by the number of its notes.

SUBSEQUENT REFERENCES

Once you have given full information for a source, you need not repeat all that information every time you cite that particular source. It used to be customary to use the Latin abbreviations "ibid.," "op. cit.," and "loc. cit." to refer to sources for which full bibliographic information had already been supplied. "Ibid." is an abbreviation for "ibidem," which means "in the same place," and it could be used when the source cited was exactly the same as the one in the note before. When the page as well as the source were the same, "ibid." was sufficient by itself, and if the page changed, the new page number could be added, as in "ibid., p. 45." Notice that if the preceding reference was several pages back, the reader, unless he remembered the source previously cited, would have to turn back to find the reference. In many cases where "ibid." appears on the same page, a judicious restatement of the text could eliminate the need for two notes.

"Op. cit." stands for "opere citato," meaning "in the work cited." "Op. cit." was used to refer to works already cited, but cited two or more footnotes back. To identify which of the preceding references was appropriate the last name of the author was given first, as in "Smith, op. cit., III, 25." If the reader does not remember the previous reference to Smith, he will probably turn to the bibliography to identify the work; if there is more than one Smith in the bibliography, or more than one work by Smith, the reader must go back through the text to find the reference. On occasion you will find an author who uses "loc. cit." for "loco citato," meaning "in the place cited." "Loc. cit." is used in place of "op. cit." when the citation is to the same page as the citation in the previous footnote in which the work was cited. "Loc. cit." guarantees the conscientious reader a search through the earlier notes.

It is now customary to use a short version of the title of a book or article instead of "op. cit." and "loc. cit." Very little space is saved by the Latin abbreviations, and the short title is not only unambiguous, but much more likely to obviate the need for a search for the full reference. Thus, instead of "Smith, op. cit., III, 25," give "Smith, *Centralia County*, III, 25." While "ibid." is still used by some authors who have abandoned "op. cit." and "loc. cit.," it too can be eliminated easily. If the second reference is several pages away from the first, surely the reader who looks down at the note will find the author's last name and a short title more informative than only "ibid." For a second reference close to the first, a minor rearrangement of the text may eliminate the need for two notes, and there is no excuse whatever for a long parade of one "ibid." after another. If you cite extensively from a single work, give the full biographical information in the first note along with a statement that subsequent references to that source will be included in the text. Thereafter, the text states the source, usually the author's name or the title of the work is enough for this, and the volume and page are placed in parentheses after the quotation or reference. The note might look like this:

[58]All references to the novel are to "The Red Badge of Courage" and Selected Prose and Poetry, ed. William M. Gibson,

Rinehart Editions 47 (New York: Rinehart & Co., 1956); page references will be included in the text.

In this example, the author of *The Red Badge of Courage*, Stephen Crane, had been named in the text. Though the article contains many references to and quotations from *The Red Badge of Courage*, this is the only reference note to the edition, since in every case the text makes clear that the quote or reference is to the novel.

CHECKING YOUR QUOTATIONS

When a scholar completes a report, he goes back to check each note. He ensures accuracy by proofreading every quotation against the original and by checking that every source says what he attributes to it at the place he cites. For a true scholar, accuracy is an end in itself. Moreover, for a publishing scholar, few things can be more devastating than a reviewer who can cite inaccuracies and factual errors. The writer of the thesis or dissertation is held to the same standards of accuracy, and his failures, if undetected by his adviser, are left in the library or on microfilm for generations of sleuths to uncover and describe in their own tomes. Although it is unlikely that reports for classes, seminars, or independent study will receive such close scrutiny, glaring inaccuracies will be detected by an alert instructor, and whatever reward the writer expected for the project will be adjusted accordingly.

Because, despite the greatest of care, mistakes creep into every scholarly work, and because the context of a quotation may change its applicability to your work, you should always check a quotation in the original work. But that is not always possible. You may find someone quoted in a source you are reading, want to use the source, but be unable to find the original work, either because it is rare and difficult to acquire or because the citation to it is incomplete. When that happens, you may use the quotation if you indicate the true source:

[41]H.G. Richardson and G. O. Sayles, The Governance of Medieval England (Edinburgh, 1963), pp. 277-78; quoted by Albert C. Baugh, "The Middle English Romance: Some Questions of Creation, Presentation, and Preservation," *Speculum*, 24 (1967), 9.

BIBLIOGRAPHIES

The last pages of the report usually contain a bibliography of some kind. The kind used should, once again, be adapted to the needs of the paper. From the writer's perspective, the easiest kind of bibliography is a list of works cited

— easiest because it requires the least thought. To compile such a bibliography you need only provide a list of all the works cited in your reference notes, all but books of the Bible and dictionaries cited in passing. However, you may choose to use a selected bibliography, for which you would evaluate your sources, whether cited in the notes or not, and select those which were most important or which might be most useful to someone who wanted to pursue the topic of the paper. If you provide comments about some of the works you include in your bibliography, then it becomes "annotated." If you want to list many items which are not in print, or if you want to include all the works you read, some of which were not cited in the notes, you might call your bibliography "List of Sources Consulted" or "List of Works Consulted," for the title of your bibliography should tell the reader what kind it is.

Whatever kind it is, it may be arranged in many ways. The simplest and most common way is to alphabetize everything in one list. Some authors, however, subdivide the list according to the kind of source. For example, frequently one finds separate, alphabetized lists for books and for articles in periodicals. Sometimes one finds separate lists for primary and secondary sources — the subdivisions might be titled "Works by Mark Twain" and "Works about Mark Twain." Such subdivisions are unnecessary for relatively short papers, where the number of sources can be easily managed in a single list. The dissertation writer who decides on subdividing his list should consult his director before committing himself to a scheme that is not in common use. Usually lists for the bibliography are alphabetically arranged. If they are not, the arrangement should be clear to the reader, and the form of entry may need to be changed to fit the scheme.

A bibliography entry includes all the information given in a full reference note except the exact pages of citations. Inclusive page numbers are given for articles in anthologies, journals, and magazines. The form of the entry in the bibliography is somewhat different from the note. First, the author's name is given last name first, since the bibliography is alphabetized according to the last name. The last name is typed next to the margin, and subsequent lines of the entry are indented, which makes it easy to find an entry in its alphabetical place. Usually, individual entries are single spaced, and double space is left between entries. If the "author" is not a person, the entry is alphabetized according to the name of the entity responsible for the work, and if the work is anonymous, it is alphabetized by the title. When the same author or entity is responsible for more than one work in the same list, a line typed ten spaces long is used in place of his name for works by him after the first one listed. The major elements of the entry are separated by periods. Thus, the basic form for a book is:

Author's last name, his first name, Name of Book. Translator or editor. Edition. Series. Volume used, or if several volumes were used, the number in the set. Place of publication: publisher, date of publication.

For a journal article, the basic form is:

Author's last name, his first name. "Title of Article." Name of Journal, volume number (date), inclusive pages of the whole article.

The Bibliography in the appendix lists, with comments in the usual place for annotations, all of the examples used for the discussion of reference notes; these examples provide models for the material usually cited in research papers.

SAMPLE BIBLIOGRAPHY

Allt, Peter and Russell K. Alspach, eds. The Variorum Edition of the Poems of W.B. Yeats, New York: The Macmillan Company, 1957.

Aristotle, Metaphysics.

This form is used when a reference to the work was made in the text but a specific edition was not cited.

Bartlett, John Russell. "Autobiography." MS in the Bartlett papers in The John Carter Brown Library, Brown University, Providence, Rhode Island.

_____ Folder marked "Dictionary" containing MS letters, notes, etc. in the Bartlett papers in The John Carter Brown Library, Brown University, Rhode Island.

The line in place of the author's name means that the first named author in this entry is the same as the first named author in the preceding entry.

Baugh, Albert C. "The Middle English Romance: Some Questions of Creation, Presentation, and Preservation." Speculum, 42 (1967), 1-31.

Bender, Marylin. "The Very Private Pritzkers: Chicago Deal Makers in Publishing Spotlight." The New York Times, October 14, 1973, Sec. 3, pp. 1 and 4.

For newspapers whose titles do not include the place of publication, that information should be added parenthetically after the title. When no volume number is given, the date is set off by commas instead of parenthesis marks.

"Beowulf"; Reproduced in Facsimile from the Unique Manuscript, British Museum MS. Cotton Vitellius A.xv. Transliteration and notes by Julius Zupitza. 2nd ed. Early English Text Society No. 245. London: Oxford University Press, 1959.

Bucy, Paul C. "Sitting on a Basketball." Paper presented at The Chicago Literary Club, April 16, 1973.

Club of Rome. The Limits of Growth: A Report for the Club of Rome's Project on the Predicament of Mankind. By Donella H. Meadows and others. New York: Universe Books, 1972.

　　　　Had Donella H. Meadows been listed as the author in the notes, then the bibliography entry would appear under that name.

Coghill, N.K. "Love and 'Foul Delight': Some Contrasted Attitudes." Patterns of Love and Courtesy: Essays in Memory of C.S. Lewis. Ed. John Lawlor. London: Edward Arnold (Publishers) Ltd., 1966, pp. 141-156.

　　　　If several of the articles in this anthology had been cited in the paper, then a single entry of the book under the editor's name would be given in the bibliography.

Crowell, Michael Gardner. "The Lexicography of Americanisms." Unpub. diss., Northwestern University, 1966.

Curtius, Ernst Robert. European Literature and the Latin Middle Ages. Trans. Willard R. Trask. The Bollingen Library. 1953; rpt. New York: Harper & Row, Publishers, 1963.

Cust, Lionel. "Gentileschi, Orazio." Dictionary of National Biography. 1908.

Dillard, Annie. "The Force that Drives the Flower." The Atlantic, 232 (November, 1973), 69-77.

Drug Abuse Survey Project. Dealing with Drug Abuse: A Report to the Ford Foundation. New York: Praeger, 1972.

Finkin, Matthew W. "Collective Bargaining and University Government." AAUP Bulletin, 57 (1971), 149-160.

Frank, Charles R., Jr., and others. Assisting Developing Countries: Problems of Debts, Burden-Sharing, Jobs and Trade. Overseas Development Council Studies 1, New York: Praeger Publishers, 1972.

"Global Annual." Anonymous rev. of The Statesman's Year-Book 1973-1974: Statistical and HIstorical Annual of the States of the World, ed. John

Paxton. The Times Literary Supplement, October 12, 1973, p. 1235.

Hueller, M.M. and others. "Hymns and Hymnals." The New Catholic Encyclopedia. 1967.

Illinois. Constitution. Article II, sec. 10.

Illinois. General Assembly. House of Representatives. High-Density Housing Committee. Report. 1970.

Illinois. General Assembly. Legislative Investigating Committee. The Drug Crisis. Report on Drug Abuse in Illinois to the Illinois General Assembly. 1971.

Illinois Revised Statutes. 1972 Supplement.

Innes, Michael [J.I.M. Stewart]. One-Man Show. New York: Dodd, Mead & Company, 1952.

Judson, Horace Freeland. "A Reporter at Large (Heroin in Great Britain — 1)." The New Yorker. September 24, 1973, pp. 76, 78-80, 85-86, 88, 93-113.

Madigan, Edward. Letter to author. September 25, 1973.

Marckwardt, Albert H. and James L. Rosier. Old English Language and Literature. New York: W.W. Norton & Company, 1972.

Meadows, Donella H. and others. The Limits of Growth: A Report for the Club of Rome's Project on the Predicament of Mankind. New York: Universe Books, 1972.

If the reference note had given "Club of Rome" as the author, then the bibliography entry would also.

Proxmire, Senator William. Speech on the appointment of Dr. William John Follner to the Council of Economic Advisors. Congressional Record, 119 (October 18, 1973), S19424-5.

An alternative form is under "U.S., Congressional Record." This citation is to the record published daily.

Renwick, W[illiam] L[indsay]. English Literature 1789-1815. Vol. IX of The Oxford History of English Literature. Ed. F[rank] P[ercy] Wilson and Bonamy Dobree. Oxford: The Clarendon Press, 1963.

If several volumes in The Oxford History were cited, a single bibliographic entry to the history would be used. See the example under "Wilson."

Richardson

> The book by Richardson was not actually used. Rather, a quotation from it was quoted from another source. That source is listed in the bibliography, instead of Richardson. See entry under "Baugh."

Sale, Roger. "England's Parnassus: C.S. Lewis, Charles Williams, and J.R.R. Tolkien." The Hudson Review, 17 (Summer, 1964), 203-225.

Sir Gawain and the Green Knight. Trans. Theodore Howard Banks, Jr. New York: Appleton-Century-Crofts, Inc., 1929.

Shakespeare, William. Hamlet.

> See comment under "Aristotle. Metaphysics."

Smith, John. The History and Tradition of Centralia County. 4 vols. Springfield, Illinois: Marigold Press, 1857-65.

> Use this form if you have used or cited more than one volume in the set.

Smith, John. The History and Tradition of Centralia County, III. Springfield, Illinois: Marigold Press, 1862.

> If you have used only one volume in a multi-volume work, cite only that volume.

Tolkien, J.R.R. "The Monsters and the Critics." Proceedings of the British Academy, 22 (1936), 245-295. Rpt. in An Anthology of Beowulf Criticism. Ed. Lewis E. Nicholson. Notre Dame, Indiana: University of Notre Dame Press, 1963.

U.S. Commission on Organization of the Executive Branch of Government (1953-1955). Paperwork Management: A Report to the Congress. Washington, D.C.: Goverment Printing Office, 1955.

U.S. Commission on Population Growth and the American Future. Governance and Population: The Governmental Amplifications of Population Change. Ed. A.E. Keir Nash. The Commission . . . Reports IV. Washington, D.C.: U.S. Government Printing Office, 1972.

U.S. Congress. House. Committee on Un-American Activities. Investigation of Communist Activities in the State of California. 11 Parts. Hearing before the Committee on Un-American Activities, 83rd Congress, 2nd session, 1954.

U.S. Congressional Record, 119 (October 18, 1973).

U.S. Constitution. Article I, sec. 3.

U.S. Department of State. Amendment of Article of Agreement of the International Finance Corporation between the U.S. of American and other Governments. Treaties and International Acts Series 7683.

U.S. Presidential Advisory Committee on Water Resources Policy. Water Resources Policy: A report. Washington, D.C. Government Printing Office, 1955.

Virgil. Aeneid.

> See comment under Aristotle.

Wilson, F[rank] P[ercy] and Bonamy, Dobree, eds. The Oxford History of English Literature. 12 vols. Oxford: The Clarendon Press, 1945-

> All of the volumes in this set have not yet been published, a fact indicated by the blank space for the closing date of publication.

APPENDIX II

SAMPLE TITLE PAGE: TERM PAPER

TWO MIDDLE ENGLISH ELEGIES

Walter Austen

English 301

Joseph Mayer

December 5, 1976

SAMPLE TITLE PAGE: DISSERTATION

BARTHOLOMEW UNIVERSITY

THE GROWTH OF LOCAL HISTORY IN THE MIDWEST

A DISSERTATION

SUBMITTED TO THE GRADUATE SCHOOL

IN PARTIAL FULFILLMENT OF THE REQUIREMENTS

for the degree

DOCTOR OF PHILOSOPHY

Field of History

By

PEREGRINE CATHERINE SPENSER

BLOOMINGTON, WISCONSIN

June 1976

APPENDIX III

SAMPLE TABLE OF CONTENTS (1)

CONTENTS

SAMPLE TABLE OF CONTENTS (2)
CONTENTS

SAMPLE TABLE OF CONTENTS (3)

CONTENTS

Profile of working mothers; historical failure to relate day care to the needs of the normal child from normal family; few working mothers use day care centers; other kinds of care.

Licensed day care homes; unlicensed day care homes; voluntary non-profit day care centers; independent proprietary day care centers; franchise centers.

Services to benefit low income families deter middle class participation in day care programs; education a popular and socially acceptable component; social service for early intervention into social and personal problems; preventive health services; corrective health service; nutritional standards for meals served in centers.

Cost; federal agencies which provide money — Department of Labor, Housing and Urban Development, Office of Economic Opportunity, Head Start, Model Cities; state aid to voluntary agencies, state aid for families in need of care; local voluntary programs.

Restrictive codes for day care homes; zoning laws which inhibit development of day care centers; standards for public health.

NOTES

NOTES

NOTES

NOTES

NOTES

NOTES

NOTES

NOTES

NOTES

NOTES